Writing in the Secondary School

Writing in the Secondary School

English and the Content Areas

Arthur N. Applebee
Stanford University

With
Anne Auten
ERIC Clearinghouse on Reading and Communication
Skills

Fran Lehr
ERIC Clearinghouse on Reading and Communication
Skills

National Council of Teachers of English
1111 Kenyon Road, Urbana, Illinois 61801

Book Design: Tom Kovacs

NCTE Stock Number 58846

The material in this publication was prepared with support in part by grant number NIE-G-79-0174 from the National Institute of Education, Department of Education. Grantees undertaking such projects under government sponsorship are encouraged to express freely their judgment in professional and technical matters. Prior to publication, the manuscript was submitted to the National Council of Teachers of English for critical review and determination of professional competence. This publication has met such standards. Points of view or opinions, however, do not necessarily represent the official view or opinions of either the National Council of Teachers of English or the National Institute of Education.

Library of Congress Cataloging in Publication Data

Applebee, Arthur N.
    Writing in the secondary school.

    (NCTE research report ; no. 21)
    Bibliography: p.
    1. English language--Composition and exercises
I. Auten, Anne. II. Lehr, Fran. III. Title.
IV. Series.
PE1011.N295 no. 21 [PE1413]   428'.007s   81-18799
ISBN 0-8141-5884-6   [428'.007'1273] AACR2

Contents

List of Tables

Acknowledgments

This study was conducted from the office of the National Council of Teachers of English and was supported in large part by a grant from the National Institute of Education. Staff of both organizations provided help at different stages of the study. In particular, Marcia Whiteman and Joseph Dominic at NIE and Robert Hogan and Bernard O'Donnell at NCTE provided personal and professional support when they were most needed.

No study of schooling can be successful without the cooperation of teachers and students. We were unusually fortunate in the cooperation, sometimes even enthusiasm, with which we were greeted in the two schools that participated in the observational studies. Both allowed us to visit classrooms throughout a full academic year. Thanks must also go to the teachers in the national sample, who took the time to complete our questionnaires and occasionally to write us lengthy letters about their teaching practices.

The success of observational studies depends upon the accuracy and perception of the observers. Fran Lehr and Anne Auten carried the brunt of the observational work; their sense of the dynamics of the classroom was essential to the success of the project.

A preliminary draft of the final report was given a detailed critique by Arthur Lehr, Champaign (Illinois) Public Schools, Robert Gundlach, Northwestern University, and Judith Langer, East Meadow (New York) Public Schools. Their comments and suggestions had a detachment of which we were no longer capable, and led to substantial changes in the presentation of results.

Finally, Kim Black, project secretary, organized us all so quietly and efficiently that we hardly noticed how complicated a task we had undertaken.

Arthur N. Applebee
Stanford University
September 1980

Foreword

As an exercise, let's propose a high school writing program certain to fail. Let's outline a program that not only thwarts students' writing development but also pointedly confuses them about how skilled writers compose and specifically precludes their gaining any insight into the ways writing can be useful to them.

How would we conduct such a perverse writing program—in all classes in the curriculum as well as in English?

We would very rarely ask students to produce original written texts of more than two or three sentences. Though students might have pencil in hand a good deal of the time, we would for the most part limit their writing to note-taking, filling in blanks in exercise books or lab manuals, writing very short responses of a phrase or at most a sentence or two to study questions or essay test questions, doing numerical calculations in math class, copying directions, or copying material from the chalkboard or from books. On the rare occasions when we did ask students to compose extended written text, we would tell them to keep it short, probably to less than a page of handwriting. We would usually request that it be finished on the spot, within just a few minutes or at most a class period. We would rarely set the due date more than two days from the time of the assignment. Students would nearly always write transactional (to convey information) discourse. We might occasionally in English class ask for fictional or personal-experience writing, but even there we would most of the time ask for informational writing. In no classes would we ask for persuasive writing. Students would write nearly always to the teacher as examiner, a reader who always knows more than they know. The purpose of the writing would be to display command of new facts or concepts or to offer proof of completion of a reading task or recollection of class lectures and discussions. Only rarely would students write to learn—to explore new insights or clarify information or examine personal experiences.

When we did ask for extended written discourse, we would limit our directions to a brief topic statement usually stated quite generally. Sometimes, especially in social science and literature classes, we would give topics about which entire books had been written by scholars in the field. We would limit our comments about the writing task to matters of length and format, and we would expect students to begin writing within two or three minutes. We would provide no help with the writing task itself. Students would have to take one

deep breath and dive in without the benefit of discussion or discovery procedures, planning and organizing, or hints about managing the drafting process
itself.

When students gave us their writing, we would take it away to read, limiting
our responses to matters of usage, spelling, and sentence structure. We would
not talk to students personally about the writing. We would not display it or
publish it. We would not ask students to read each other's writing. On the few
occasions when we asked students to revise their writing, we would be satisfied
with small corrections and additions.

It will surprise and dismay many people to learn that the sober, cautious,
sophisticated research study reported in this monograph demonstrates that the
writing program I have just described is the standard program in American high
schools. Even the bright and promising exceptions to the standard program—
and they are documented as well in this report—do not alter this grim conclusion. With some luck high school students will encounter a history or science
teacher who knows that writing is a way to learn history or science, not just a
way to report what has been learned. Students just may chance upon an
English teacher who writes and who understands the writing process, who
cares as much about students' writing development as about their acquaintance
with particular literary texts. All students will now and then confront a chal-
lenging writing assignment, a long, complex, and intriguing one; and they will
learn something for themselves from it about writing and what writing can do.
But usually, most days, month after month, it's the standard program.

Members of the Committee on Research of the National Council of Teachers
of English take no pleasure in the findings of this study, but we take great
pride in including the report itself in our Research Report series. This report,
authored by the distinguished educational researcher and historian Arthur
Applebee, is Number 21 in a series dating back to 1963. Barely a study a year
from many submissions is considered good enough for publication in the series.
The purpose of the series is to report research findings of interest to school
and college English teachers and to provide models of the best current research
designs and approaches to data analysis.

Arthur Applebee's report, *Writing in the Secondary Schools: English and
the Content Areas,* is a model survey study. It is impressive in its comprehen-
siveness and thoroughness. It includes painstaking observational work in classrooms, interviews with students and teachers, and wide-scale surveying with a
questionnaire. The report reminds us once again of the value of skillful surveys.
So far all the evidence for a writing crisis has come from student writing or
from various indirect measures like the verbal aptitude test of the Scholastic
Achievement Test. Now Applebee takes us inside classrooms and shows us
what is going on in writing instruction, not just in English classes, but in
math, social science, science, foreign language, and business classes. Looking

at his results, we can easily believe there must be a writing crisis, even if we had doubted it until now. We might conclude, too, that American high school graduates who have experienced only the standard program are writing better than we have a right to expect. Even as we point to the very real institutional constraints in American high schools—poor working conditions for teachers, crowded classes—we can still acknowledge the school-based causes of the writing crisis: lack of writing and poor instruction.

For the Research Report series Applebee's arresting report is unusual in the force of its implications for instruction, a forcefulness made possible by the wide-spread consensus on what a good high school writing program should look like. Knowing that consensus, Applebee confidently outlines the elements and practices of a good program, one that encourages all students' writing development by assuring that they all gain some control of the composing process and some knowledge of the many uses of writing for thinking, learning, and personal development. Because of the care and thoroughness of his study, his sound proposals are sure to command attention.

Charles R. Cooper
Committee on Research
National Council of Teachers of English

1 Introduction

The last several years have seen an increased interest in the writing process and in the teaching of writing. Prompted in part by public concern about the state of the nation's literacy, the new interest is apparent in the College Entrance Examination Board's restoration of a writing sample to its examinations, in the inclusion of composition as an area eligible for funding in the 1978 amendments to the Elementary and Secondary Education Act, and in the increased funding of projects to investigate writing and writing instruction through the National Institute of Education.

This public concern with writing skills has coincided with new insights into the linguistic and psychological processes involved in writing—insights drawn from a range of disciplines using a variety of research techniques.

Case studies have become especially popular, sparked largely by Emig's (1971) analysis of the writing processes of twelfth grade students and Graves's (1973) work in elementary school classrooms. But we have also had rigorous experimental studies (Bereiter and Scardamelia, in press), detailed ethnographic research (Florio, 1978), and large-scale assessments of students' ability to respond to particular writing tasks (NAEP, 1975; 1976; 1977a, b; 1980 a, b, c). In a different tradition, linguists and rhetoricians have developed new approaches to the study of texts, moving beyond the sentence level toward descriptions of the structures underlying a text as a whole (Kinneavy, 1971; Halliday and Hasan, 1976), and psychologists have begun to study propositional structures in their relationship to comprehension (Freedle, 1979).

Most of this recent work grows out of highly specialized contexts, defined either by the constraints of a particular academic discipline or by the dynamics of a particular set of classrooms and teachers who have become excited about writing and who have the advantage of continuing interaction with an equally enthusiastic researcher. Ultimately, the findings of such research will have to be integrated with our knowledge of the conditions under which writing is usually taught; we will have to work our way out of the specialized contexts toward an understanding of what would be most feasible and most fruitful in classrooms in general.

Relating new research to current practice is no easy matter, however, for in spite of a general discontent with the results of writing instruction very little is known about the writing that school children do. Are they writing at all?

Are the tasks appropriate and productive? Does writing instruction vary from teacher to teacher and subject to subject? Do variations in instruction in fact matter? If so, in what ways?

The present study, growing out of such questions, seeks to portray in some detail the instructional situations within which students are presently learning to write. Data of a variety of sorts were gathered in order to describe as fully as possible (1) the nature of the writing tasks currently being asked of secondary school students; (2) teachers' purposes and techniques in making writing assignments; and (3) the extent to which the characteristics of student writing vary with the subject area, grade level, and instructional goals.

In its approach to these questions, the present study is itself embedded within a larger research tradition that assumes that whatever else writing may be, it is fundamentally a language process. As such, much that we have learned about language in general remains relevant in our discussion of learning to write and provides us with powerful frames of reference to sort out what we know, to help relate isolated facts one to another, and to reveal where the significant gaps in our knowledge lie.

To take one example, it has become a cliché to assert, "writing is difficult." Yet if we examine this assertion at all carefully, it is clear that there is nothing about writing *itself* that is difficult. Even young children just learning to write find very little that is difficult about it. They write, typically, with great pleasure, and they write everywhere: floors, walls, and table tops are just as likely as their writing tables to bear the brunt of their excursions into written language. It is only in certain specialized contexts that writing becomes difficult for them, as when they are asked to write for their teacher, clearly and between the lines. Not writing itself, but writing to meet the demands of a particular task complicates the process.

This is also true at other levels on the developmental scale. The adolescent who finds it almost impossible to write a history report will compose effortless notes to pass to classmates when the teacher's back is turned. The scholar who labors endlessly over a particular chapter will seize the chance to write a lengthy letter to a friend about how the manuscript is developing. Again, it is the nature of the writing task, not writing itself, that complicates the process.

The argument is more complex, however, than the simple assertion that particular uses of language (and hence of writing as a form of language) are difficult and others are not. Writing is distinguishable in certain formal ways from spoken language, particularly in providing a permanent record that can be reflected upon, edited, and preserved. These formal differences provide in fact new language resources which are not readily available in spoken contexts. These resources have led in turn to the development of new ways of using language which exist almost exclusively in writing, and which are embedded within certain highly specialized social and academic disciplines. It is from these new and specialized tasks—which demand what David Olson (1977) has called "essayist technique"—that we derive the belief that "writing" is difficult, forgetting that there are many other uses of writing which do not seem to be difficult at all.

Describing Writing

Discussions of the "difficulty" of writing go astray when they neglect to treat writing as language with a variety of possible uses. "Use" in fact turns out to be an equally critical factor in just about any other aspect of writing one cares to examine, from testing and evaluation to modelling the composing process to comparing teaching techniques. Thus in a study of school writing it becomes important to have a coherent approach to discussing and distinguishing among the universes of possible uses of language in general and of writing in particular. There are a variety of perspectives that can be taken in examining uses of language, but two that are particularly helpful and complementary are those of Michael Halliday and James Britton. For our purposes, Halliday provides a way to conceptualize the conventions of particular genres, while Britton offers a framework for examining across-genre similarities in language tasks.

Halliday's (1977; and Hasan, 1976) discussions of the uses of language focus attention on language at the level of text, where text is a general term for a semantic structure formed out of a continuous process of choice among interrelated sets of semantic options, in speech or writing. The importance of text as a formal construct is that it moves us immediately beyond the level of the individual sentence and asks us to examine the characteristics of larger stretches of discourse. This has a number of aspects. One relates to formal characteristics of a text, ways of beginning and ending, for example, as well as to the sorts of differences that emerge if you compare the Modern Language Association *Style Sheet* with the American Psychological Association *Publication Manual.* Some of these differences are relatively trivial, related mostly to fine tuning a manuscript. Other text differences, however, provide crucial signals about the sort of task that is being undertaken, conventional markers which we do not notice simply because they work so well. An author of a scientific paper *cannot* begin, "Once upon a time," any more than an editorial writer can indulge in a formal review of related literature.

Another aspect of text is the mode of organization of meaning—that is, the way the parts of the text relate to one another, which includes such features as cohesion, propositional structure, and narrative sequence. As scholars have turned their attention to such characteristics, it has become increasingly clear that an important part of any well-formed text involves decisions about what is necessary and appropriate to make explicit, and what should be left implicit. The issue is pervasive, from pronominal reference through the problem of which procedures can simply be cited and which must be explained in detail in a scholarly report. Halliday introduces the concept of register to deal with some of these problems, defining register as a particular configuration of semantic options associated with a particular context of use. Decisions about which options to choose are decisions about the appropriate realization in written language of the "paradigms" Thomas Kuhn (1962) has discussed as the foundation of particular fields of scientific inquiry. These paradigms provide tacit guidelines about proper lines of evidence and modes of argument. Though rarely made explicit, their influence is pervasive; they determine what will be seen as interesting, what as obvious, and what as needing elaboration. When we move beyond remedial or "basic" English, problems in managing this aspect of text are the cause of much that we call poor writing.

Doctoral dissertations provide a familiar example of such problems. Typically, the candidate reaches the dissertation stage with an overwhelming array of new information, new ideas, new terminology—and with great excitement about it all. What is most often lacking is a sense of what is significant and what is trivial. The manuscript that results often verges on incoherence, with important findings swamped by details of interest only to the student who has just discovered them. We get long explanations of standard techniques, table after table of statistical findings, page after page of explanations that a more experienced scholar knows can be taken for granted, or saved for another report with a different purpose. It is the failure to adequately come to terms with the tacit knowledge of the field that keeps even many of the most significant doctoral studies from being publishable, however much the unpublished dissertation becomes a standard citation in later reviews of the field.

In looking at the writing of secondary school students in the present study, one of our assumptions is that major subject areas represent differing universes of discourse, each with characteristic registers and differentiated writing skills. But we also suspect that teachers may sometimes undercut the development of those specialized skills without realizing it. Very early in our work, for example, we found that when students were asked to write within the conventions of particular subject areas, the teacher tended to take over the responsibility for insuring that the text was appropriate. They did this in various ways, but the most obvious was the short-answer or multiple-choice response format, where the teacher structured the language, and the student had nothing to do but "slot" information into place. This is a very efficient way to go about some teaching tasks, but it is questionable how much it helps students learn to construct texts appropriate to the discipline involved.

Halliday's work provides a way to conceptualize the specialized writing skills associated with particular disciplines and contexts of use. In turning instead to examine dimensions of writing that cut across the various contexts, our starting point is James Britton's (1970; et al., 1975) analyses of school writing in a variety of subject areas in British secondary schools. He describes two dimensions of these tasks in some detail: one relates to the audience for the writing and the other to the function of the text, where function is used in the sense of the conventional purpose the text is designed to accomplish (tell a story, report an event, persuade, or theorize).

At one level, Britton's analysis of audience is a traditional one, tailored to fit the specific audiences that students encounter in the course of their school work. Categories he investigates begin with "child to self," range through specialized school categories such as "pupil to examiner," and end in "writers to their (unknown) readers." As might be expected, virtually all of the writing that Britton and his colleagues (1975) collected from British schools was addressed to the teacher, and the greater proportion was addressed to the teacher in the role of examiner.

In the present study, we began by looking at both the *actual* audience for student writing, and the *purported* audience in the "write a letter to the mayor" type of assignment. Even with this distinction, it is difficult to do much that is interesting with audience in an observational study because there is little variability: virtually all of the writing that is done is really done for the teacher. Compared with writing in out-of-school contexts, this is a very atypical audience: on most assigned topics, the teacher not only knows more about the topic than does the student writer, but wants the student to repeat what has already been said. In this context, teachers may be tempted to treat unclear prose gently, supplying missing information and reading for what the student "meant to say." Something of this sort probably happens with the doctoral dissertations discussed earlier; they pass easily through dissertation committees who know what the candidate "meant to say," but not through publishers' review boards, which concentrate on what the manuscript actually says. Douglas Barnes (1976) has commented on the lack of demand inherent in writing for someone who understands in advance, arguing that speakers and writers order their thoughts more carefully when addressing uninformed audiences than when addressing well-informed ones. This is similar to the claim in Britton's work that when audiences other than the teacher existed—or were created through the intervention of the project team—both involvement with the writing task and the quality of the writing that resulted improved noticeably (see Martin et al., 1976).

It is here that this approach to audience parts company with the traditional concern with matching what you say to what you know about your reader, and becomes part of a more general (and more interesting) argument about the way in which we learn language. Briefly stated, the argument is that language is learned most naturally and most effectively through use, and that the most significant uses are driven by intention to communicate. When we create writing situations with atypical audiences, we destroy the normal intention to communicate and thus undermine in fundamental ways the whole learning process.

In analyzing the function or "use" of language, Britton begins with a split which is essentially between literary and expository text. He takes this traditional starting point, however, and reformulates it in terms of the relationship between the language user and the language experience; like Halliday, he focuses our attention on the semantic purpose of the text, rather than on its surface linguistic features. On the one hand, there is language that is concerned with objectivity and task fulfillment, whether that task relates to the exigencies of day-to-day living ("Place your order here") or to the complications of theory-building and professional discourse. Britton calls language used in these ways *transactional,* since it is the basis for objective exchange of information and argument in our transactions with one another. On the other hand, there is language that invites the reader to "live through" an experience and to construct a personal, essentially subjective interpretation of it. Such language differs from the transactional in that the represented experience becomes important in itself, rather than the representation being used as a tool toward some other end. Following Aristotle, Britton calls language used in this way *poetic,* and includes within it the whole spectrum of literary genres.

There are a number of subdivisions in Britton's model, the most useful of which form an abstractive scale underlying expository prose—an instance of Britton's transactional uses of language. The subcategories here are an elaboration of a set proposed by Moffett (1968); they range from a simple report of ongoing experience to tautological argument in which the conclusions reached are in one sense fully entailed within the premises from which the text begins. Movement along this scale of abstraction involves movement through a series of differing, and increasingly formalized and explicit, systems of logic.

In his studies of secondary school writing, Britton found characteristic differences in the level of abstraction emphasized in different subject areas and at different grade levels. He found almost no writing, in any subject, that moved beyond essentially classificatory types of writing.

For the present study we began with Britton's work, extending and adapting his categories for our own purposes. The system that resulted is presented in chapter 3.

The Instructional Context

Though having systematic ways to describe student writing was a necessary first step in our work, it is also true that being able to describe completed writing tells us little about how the writer achieved that form. A simple one-page report of a science experiment, for example, could represent a wide range of different activities: a one-shot exercise completed by a student who understood the instructions; the last in a long series of similar reports, each discussed and refined by the teacher; or a formula piece, where students were given a line-by-line framework to fill in with the details of a particular experiment. The completed writing could also represent anything from a first quick draft to a carefully rewritten piece incorporating teacher comments and corrections.

The present study sought to explore such differences by investigating the instructional context within which students were being asked to write. This context has many facets, including writing frequency, steps insisted upon in the writing task (research, review, prewriting, first drafts, revisions, editing, peer-criticism, teachers' reactions, and so on), and teachers' emphases in marking.

Frequency of writing is probably the easiest aspect of writing instruction to measure, and is obviously important. Still, we have no carefully collected data about the frequency or nature of writing tasks required of the typical American secondary school student, though some information is available about highly select groups. In a study of winners in the NCTE Achievement Awards in Writing competition, for example, we found that about 80 percent of the students were doing some paragraph-length writing for English each week (Applebee, 1978b). Although English accounted for a larger portion of the required writing than did any other single subject area, it still accounted for less than half of the writing the students were doing. This contributed to our decision to examine, as part of the present study, the nature of the writing required in a variety of subject areas. (The demands may be sharply contrasting: compare the poem written in response to a film during an English lesson with the essay on 'sportsmanship' given as a disciplinary measure by the physical education teacher. Each assignment contributes in its own way to students' attitudes toward writing and to their ultimate writing proficiency.)

In twelfth grade English, the essay on literary topics represented over half of the continuous writing completed by the award-winning students; creative or imaginative writing represented 23 percent, an apparent increase over proportions found during the 1960s (Squire and Applebee, 1968). Both frequency of writing and topics for writing varied significantly with such factors as class size and type of curriculum (for example, nontraditional electives versus English IV). Similarly, large variations could be expected between the experiences of those award-winning, highly motivated students and those of more typical students.

In conceptualizing our approach to other aspects of instruction, we turned again to studies of language use and language development. Halliday (1977), in discussing the development of language skills in his son Nigel, illustrated how as an infant Nigel structured his first simple narratives in interaction with adults. In one example, Nigel returned from the zoo and began to talk with his father (and later his mother) about an incident in which a goat had tried to eat a plastic garbage pail lid:

N.   try eat lid
F.   What tried to eat the lid?
N.   try eat lid
F.   What tried to eat the lid?
N.   goat . . . man said no . . . goat try to eat lid . . . man said no

Then, after a further interval, while being put to bed:

N.   goat try eat lid . . . man said no
M.   Why did the man say no?
N.   goat shouldn't eat lid . . . (shaking head) good for it
M.   The goat shouldn't eat the lid; it's not good for it.
N.   goat try eat lid . . . man said no . . . goat shouldn't eat lid . . .
     (shaking head) good for it

This story is then repeated as a whole, verbatim, at frequent inter-
vals over the next few months. (Halliday, 1977; p. 112)

Among the interesting features of this interaction are (1) that it relies on a
skill which the child has already developed (dialogue) to develop a new skill
(narrative); (2) that the help is provided to accomplish a task that the child
wishes to accomplish but cannot successfully accomplish on his own; and (3)
that the help is gradually withdrawn as the child becomes capable of sustaining
this level of discourse on his own. The process is a very general one in language
learning; it provides a *scaffold* (Bruner, 1978) or support that allows the child
to engage in a task that would otherwise be too difficult while also learning a
general procedure which eventually makes the support unnecessary.

Cazden (1980) has pointed out that the "scaffold" in such a situation is a
very unusual scaffold indeed, one that "self-destructs gradually as the need
lessens, and is then replaced by a new structure for a more elaborate construc-
tion." Basing her discussion both on studies of language learning in the home
and on studies of classroom discourse, Cazden comments:

> Ideally, it seems to me, one would hope to find opportunities
> for children to practice a growing range of discourse functions—
> explaining, narrating, instructing, etc.—first in situations in which
> a scaffold or model of some appropriate kind is available, and then
> gradually with less and less help. Such opportunities should be
> especially important for practice in the various kinds of extended
> monologues that children are expected to write in assigned themes.

The concept of instructional "scaffolding" or support provided us with a very
powerful way to look at the teaching of writing, particularly when it was combined with an analysis of writing as a process which varies from task to task
and which poses differing problems for the writer at different points in time.

In the ideal instructional situation, we would expect that students would
gradually take on more difficult writing tasks, with appropriate instructional
support that would in turn gradually be withdrawn. Though we found little
that approximated this ideal, we remain convinced that differences in the ex-

tent and nature of the instructional scaffolding or support provided may well be the most significant differences in teachers' approaches to writing.

Design of the Study

In order to develop as rich a portrait as possible of current practice within the constraints of budgets and time, two related strands of research were planned. The first strand involved classroom observations of writing assignments and related instruction in two midwestern high schools, over a full academic year. This strand was designed to give us a detailed picture of the place of writing in the schools, without the complications introduced by self-report data. We were able to study in some detail the attitudes and practices of particular teachers in a variety of subject areas and to examine students' reactions to the writing they were asked to do. Because the data were gathered through classroom observation, we also had the opportunity to sharpen our sense of the questions we wanted to ask, refining our hypotheses about significant dimensions of variation in instruction.

Observations based on two schools, however extensive, remain essentially case studies of particular situations. To relate what we were observing to more general practice, the second strand of the study involved a national questionnaire survey of teachers in six major subject areas: English, foreign language, mathematics, science, social science, and business education. Though the data in this strand are limited to what teachers said they were doing, the responses did reflect their attitudes about good practice, and allowed us to investigate how these attitudes varied with such factors as subject area and grade level.

Overview of the Report

In the report that follows, results from the various parts of the study are woven together around the major research topics: the types of writing students are asked to do, teachers' purposes in making these assignments, and the interaction of purposes with the writing instruction provided. Chapter 6 brings the major findings together in one place, summarizing the results in outline form. The final chapter places the results in the context of the more general question of what is needed to improve writing instruction in the secondary school. In service of the same goal, Appendix 2 provides a bibliography of materials that offer practical, classroom-oriented suggestions for incorporating writing into a variety of different subject areas.

2 Procedures

The design of the study incorporated both observational studies and a national questionnaire survey. The observational studies, which began in October 1979, concentrated on the nature and frequency of situations in which students were being asked to write in all subject areas. For most of the observations, the individual lesson was taken as the sampling unit, with random observations of regular class instruction scheduled throughout the academic year.

A few additional lesson sequences were observed in order to trace the unfolding of writing episodes over sequences of related lessons. Because these lesson sequences were not randomly selected, they are drawn upon only anecdotally in the discussions that follow; they were not included in the statistical analyses.

The national questionnaire survey concentrated on six major subject areas. By gathering information from a larger and more representative sample, it allowed us to relate specific findings from the observational studies to more general practice in American schools.

Observational Studies

The major instrument developed for the observational studies was a simple log of class activities with space to note time to the nearest minute (read from a digital display). The central section of the log-sheet was used to describe the types of class activities observed (class discussion, teacher presentation, transition between activities), as well as any writing or note-taking activities. Time was recorded whenever activities changed or were interrupted. During periods of whole-class discussion, occurrences of teacher or pupil questions were also recorded.

After a lesson ended, observers used the information on the log to code the occurrence and duration of various activities; coding instructions and full definitions of measures are included in Applebee et al. (1980).

In addition to the coded data derived from each observation, observers prepared brief accounts of the significant elements in the lesson as a whole. The nature of these accounts varied depending upon the lesson, but the focus was on teacher and pupil expectations, as reflected in the patterns of interaction and social relationships apparent during the observations. (Specific

11

examples, including teacher-pupil dialogue, were noted on the log of activities.) These accounts provided many examples useful in interpreting empirical results and were a rich source of hypotheses for later exploration.

Because we sought the cooperation of teachers in the two schools over the whole academic year, observation procedures minimized demands on teacher time. The major request made by the study was to be allowed into the classroom; beyond that point, observers gathered the data without intruding further. When student writing was observed, however, observers asked to borrow the set of papers; a random sample of six scripts was then photocopied for later analysis, and the originals were returned to the teacher. Scripts, logs of observations, and code sheets were identified by code number; teachers' and students' names were removed whenever they occurred.

Sample

Two schools were selected for the observational studies after meetings with the principals, department heads, and teachers involved. One school was selected as a relatively typical city high school, serving a diverse population with a range of goals; the other, a university-run laboratory school, was selected to provide as sharp a contrast as possible in instructional goals and practices.

The original research design called for observations of ninth and twelfth grade classes, the extremes of the senior high school years. Discussions with department heads at the laboratory school, however, made it clear that many seniors took university classes, and that instruction during the spring tended to be atypical, with a change of emphasis and activities after college entrance had been assured. Because of this, the focus in the study as a whole was shifted to ninth and eleventh grade classes.

The Laboratory School

The laboratory school is associated with a large state university in the midwest and exists to assist in the research, training, and service activities of the university's curriculum laboratory and college of education. Admission is competitive (there are three or more applicants for each opening) and is limited to 250 students in five grades. Students selected for admission must have ranked in the top 10 percent of their classes as measured by standardized group tests. In addition, they are tested by the school before acceptance.

Most students enter the school following their sixth grade year and are placed in a combined seventh/eighth grade (subfreshman) class. While the student body is racially and ethnically mixed, this mix is due largely to the international make up of the university (with which many of the students' parents are associated). Students are not required to pay tuition. The school emphasizes the fields of English, science, mathematics, languages, social studies, and the arts, and course offerings are limited in number. Approximately 95 percent of the graduating students continue their formal education.

All twenty teachers of ninth and eleventh grade classes agreed to participate in the study. The participating teachers were from mathematics (5), foreign language (7), social studies (3), English (2), and science (3).

City High School

The city high school participating in the study is one of three public high schools located in a midwestern community of approximately 95,000. The school serves some 1,400 students in four grades. The school population is racially and ethnically mixed (79.3 percent white, 20.7 percent minority) and represents a true cross section of the community as well as a diverse group of interests and needs.

It is a comprehensive school and students may choose from a wide variety of vocational or college preparatory courses. The school also serves special education and educable mentally handicapped students. Most courses are one semester in length and students must register for five academic classes and physical education each semester. To graduate, students must accumulate either sixteen (class of 1980) or eighteen (classes after 1980) credits, including three credits in English, one and a half in physical education, one in social studies, one half in health, one half in consumer education, and (for classes after 1980) two in mathematics and science.

Deliberate ability-level grouping occurs only in ninth grade English. Based on their performance in the middle schools, on teacher recommendations, and on standardized testing, entering students are placed in either a high, average, or low section of this course. Low sections have fewer students than higher sections and students receive more individualized attention. Grouping in other areas is not deliberate but occurs through a student's choice of courses (biology over life science, algebra over general mathematics). Approximately 60 percent of the graduating students of this school continue their formal education.

Of the sixty teachers at the appropriate grade levels, forty-eight agreed to participate in the study. Eight declined to participate at all, two had student teachers who did not wish to be visited, and two had classes that were regularly out of the building as part of work-study and career education programs. The participating teachers were from English (11), foreign language (4), science (5), social studies (4), mathematics (4), business education (6), art (2), industrial arts (7), home economics (1), and special education (4).

Classes Observed

Observations of randomly selected ninth and eleventh grade classes began in October 1979 and continued through April 1980. In all, 309 lessons were observed during twenty-five weeks of school. Of these, 259 observations fell within the main sampling frame. The remaining lessons included 22 repeated observations to provide a check of observer reliability, 12 representing unusual grade level or subject area combinations (e.g., a personal typing class with students from all four high school grades), and 16 chosen to look at lesson sequences of particular interest. Table 1 summarizes the number of classes observed in each subject at each grade level as part of the primary sample. English classes, where we expected to find more writing activities, were deliberately oversampled. Subject areas included under "other" include a range of practical and applied courses, particularly in the areas of industrial arts, domestic science, and art.

The number of observations of any given teacher varied, depending upon subject area, the number of participating teachers at the grade levels sampled, and the outcome of the random selection of classes. Over the course of the year, the number of observations for each teacher ranged from 1 to 11, with an average of 3.5 at the city high school and 4.7 at the laboratory school.

Profiles of Class Activities

The way a teacher typically organizes a lesson to some extent delimits the writing that will be observed. Except for note-taking, for example, we would expect to find little writing during class discussions. Tables 26 and 27, Appendix 1, provide a detailed summary of the types of activities observed during classroom visits. At the laboratory school, the major activity was teacher-led class discussion; this accounted for an average of 41 percent of the class time.

Table 1

Observations Completed

Subject Area	Laboratory School		City High School		Totals
	Grade 9	Grade 11	Grade 9	Grade 11	
English	9	9	16	22	56
Foreign Language	8	11	11	6	36
Math	10	8	12	7	37
Science	10	9	8	11	38
Social Science	10	9	10	9	38
Business Education			0	17	17
Special Education			5	9	14
Other			5	18	23
Totals	47	46	67	99	259

(For the most part, teacher-led was also teacher-dominated discussion; teachers asked 70.3 percent of the questions during such discussions at the laboratory school, and 77.5 percent at the city high school.) Another 15 percent of time was spent taking tests or correcting exercises, 12 percent on group work, and 9 percent on seat work with individual students working on their own. The pattern at the city high school was somewhat different. Only an average of 28 percent of class time was spent on teacher-led class discussion and only 4 percent on group work. Instead there was more emphasis on individual seat work, which accounted for 31 percent of class time.

Class sizes at the city high school averaged 18.8, significantly higher than the 16.0 observed at the laboratory school. Correlations with patterns of class activities were slight, however. At the city high school, time spent on individual seat work actually increased slightly as classes got smaller ($r = -.13$, $p < .05$), reflecting the popularity of such work in small remedial classes. Pooling the two samples, time spent on teacher presentation was likely to increase ($r = .10$, $p < .05$) and pupil-led discussion to decrease ($r = -.12$, $p < .03$) as class sizes went up. The only relatively strong relationship between class activities and class size occurred for the time spent on administration and transition; it increased ($r = .21$, $p < .001$) as the number of students to be managed increased.

Observer Bias

Placing an observer in a classroom inevitably alters the classroom climate to some degree. In the present study, teachers were aware that our overall concern was with student uses of writing, and were always told of planned observations at least a day in advance. This gave them the opportunity to ask us not to come to a particular lesson, or to place more emphasis on writing than might otherwise have occurred. Occasionally, it was clear that one or the other of these biases did occur. Students asked to take notes in one social science class were plainly puzzled by the request, and wanted to know why this new task was being demanded; others in a German class, though cooperative and eager, were caught unprepared when asked to write out their answers to oral exercises, and had to ask for paper; the teacher in an English literature class suddenly shifted ground and asked students to write about how they write papers— because, as she told us later, she thought we would be interested in what the students had to say. (We were.)

A few such instances notwithstanding, the teachers and students soon seemed used to our presence, and went about their usual tasks in their usual ways. The relatively low incidence of writing and related activities in the lessons observed (see chapter 3) suggests that very few of the teachers were trying to show us what they thought we wanted to see.

National Questionnaire Survey

The questionnaire for the national survey was developed in three stages. A first version of the questionnaire, based in part on earlier surveys (Applebee, 1978a, b) and in part on first-semester results from the observational studies, was circulated for criticism among staff members, English department heads, and selected outside experts in the field of composition. From their reactions, a revised version was prepared for piloting in the schools cooperating in the observational studies. All sixty-eight participating teachers were asked to complete this pilot version; sixty-seven completed questionnaires were returned and analyzed.

The questionnaire was organized into a number of sets of related questions. It focused on such areas as goals for writing instruction, marking practices, methods of structuring assignments, audiences for student writing, and the nature and frequency of writing assignments. Initial analyses of the various subsets of questions revealed a tendency for each to be dominated by the teacher's estimate of the overall importance of writing to his or her particular subject area, though some secondary patterns of response were also evident after removing this general "importance of writing" factor. For the final version of the questionnaire, questions were revised to separate "importance of writing" from other attitudes, and to provide more balanced sampling of items related to the various secondary patterns that emerged from the analyses. (Discussions of the specific nature of these patterns, as well as of the extent to which they held up in moving from the pilot to the main sample, are included in the presentation of results.)

The final version of the questionnaire was largely self-coding, but a small number of open-ended questions sampling general attitudes were also included. In addition, teachers with classes in which any writing of at least paragraph length was required were asked to include photocopies of two papers: one from the top quarter and one from the bottom quarter of those received in response to a recent assignment. Students' names and other identifying information were removed from all samples, and teachers could indicate if they preferred that the papers not be quoted in reporting results from the survey. A copy of the questionnaire is included in Applebee et al. (1980).

Sample Selection

A two-stage sampling procedure was used for the national survey; a number of steps were taken to insure that the response rate would be high and the sample representative.

First, buildings containing ninth graders and those containing eleventh graders were separately sampled from the population of all public schools nationally. The sample was stratified by metropolitan status (metropolitan area, urban fringe, or rural) using U.S. Census categorizations (Bureau of the Census, 1978) and by school size. Within cells, samples were randomly drawn with sampling fractions proportionate to total enrollment.

Second, principals received individually typed and signed requests for assistance; these letters pointed out that only about one hundred schools at the grade level sampled were being asked to participate, and hence that each response was especially important. To insure that questionnaire responses would represent "good practice" in each of the subject areas, principals were asked to nominate six competent teachers to participate in the survey, one each for English, science, social science, mathematics, foreign language, and business education. The teachers were to be selected on the basis of their competence in teaching their own subjects, rather than for special interest in student writing. Principals were given the option of replying by mail or being contacted later by telephone if they wished more information before deciding whether to participate. To personalize the survey as much as possible, initial and reply envelopes were hand stamped.

Third, nominated teachers were addressed by name, and received letters tailored to their particular subject area. The letters pointed out that they had been nominated as "good teachers" by their principal and that the small number of schools being asked to participate made each response particularly important. In addition, a new one dollar bill was included with each questionnaire, as a token of the importance placed on the response and to defray expenses for postage and for photocopying the writing samples that were requested. Responses were identified only by school code numbers.

Fourth, because teaching practices and attitudes toward writing may vary from class to class even for a particular teacher, each teacher was asked to report on a single class in the appropriate subject at the sampled grade level. The class to be reported on was randomly selected by project staff on the basis of principals' reports of the number of eligible classes taught by that teacher. Instructions to teachers were phrased in terms of the "first/second/ . . . /last" such class met each day.

Response Rates

The initial sample of buildings within cells in the sampling frame was drawn by Market Data Retrieval, Inc., from their comprehensive lists of U.S. schools. Problems involved in obtaining a research sample from lists designed primarily for high-volume commercial mailings delayed the start of the survey, and meant that sampling of teachers continued until the end of the academic year—when pressures of exams, final reports, and summer vacations were at their height.

Nonetheless, response rates were good. Of the 235 building principals contacted, 196, or 83 percent, nominated teachers to participate. (Eleven others agreed to participate but did not follow through with nominations of specific teachers.) Response rates were relatively constant across cells, except for a fluctuation related to building size in the ninth grade sample. Principals who did not allow their schools to participate cited a variety of reasons; the most frequent were policies limiting participation to district-sponsored studies, the end-of-year crush in districts that close relatively early, and an unwillingness to burden teachers with any additional tasks. Response rates by school size and metropolitan area are summarized in table 2.

The 196 building principals nominated a total of 1,108 teachers to receive the questionnaires. Of these, 754, or 68 percent, responded with useable questionnaires before the closing date of July 1, 1980. The responses represented classes taught over a fourteen week period in the spring of 1980. Again, response rates were relatively constant across cells of the design, with the lowest rate of response from eleventh grade foreign language teachers (49 percent) and the highest from ninth grade English teachers (78 percent). Response rates by school size, metropolitan area, and subject are summarized in table 3.

In addition to completing the questionnaire, teachers were asked to provide two samples of student writing in response to a recent assignment, if samples were available. Overall, 28 percent of the teachers provided the samples requested, but there were large subject-area differences in response rates (table 4).

Characteristics of Participating Teachers and Schools

Tables 5 and 6 summarize a number of general characteristics of the participating schools and teachers, as well as of the particular classes upon which the teachers were asked to report.

Schools in metropolitan areas, which have the largest proportion of students, were most heavily represented in the sample; similarly, the number of schools sampled within each enrollment range was proportional to the number of students and teachers represented, rather than to the number of separate buildings in the sampled population. The four major census regions were relatively equally represented at grade nine, though at grade eleven the west was somewhat underrepresented and the south was overrepresented. The percent of students eventually going on to some form of higher education averaged just under 50 percent; the percent of nonwhite minorities, just over 10 percent.

The general characteristics of the participating teachers and classes suggest that they were indeed somewhat better than average, as should have been the case since principals were asked to nominate "good" teachers. Classes with below average (including special education) students were markedly undersampled, representing only 12 percent of the classes at grade nine and 4 percent at grade eleven. The teachers tended to have more experience than would be expected in a random sample, averaging twelve and fourteen years for the ninth and eleventh grade samples, respectively. Over a fourth of the sampled teachers had supervisory responsibilities over other teachers (for example, as department head or team leader).

Table 2

Rate of Participation: Schools

Schools	Grade 9			Grade 11		
	Number Contacted	Number Participating	Response Rate (%)	Number Contacted	Number Participating	Response Rate (%)
Metropolitan status						
Metropolitan area	65	53	81.5	50	41	82.0
Urban fringe	26	20	76.9	26	21	80.8
Rural	34	29	85.3	34	32	94.1
Enrollment range						
Under 500	14	8	57.1	11	10	90.9
500–999	53	48	90.6	46	38	82.6
1000–2499	46	39	84.7	38	34	89.5
2500+	12	7	58.3	15	12	80.0
All	125	102	81.6	110	94	85.5

Table 3

Rate of Participation: Teachers

Teachers	Grade 9			Grade 11		
	Number Contacted	Number Participating	Response Rate (%)	Number Contacted	Number Participating	Response Rate (%)
Metropolitan status						
Metropolitan area	293	207	70.6	242	163	67.4
Urban fringe	107	74	69.2	125	73	58.4
Rural	149	107	71.8	192	130	67.7
Enrollment range						
Under 500	39	27	69.2	49	37	75.5
500–999	259	195	75.3	228	149	65.4
1000–2499	211	141	66.8	204	129	63.2
2500+	40	25	62.5	78	51	65.4
Subject area						
English	102	80	78.4	94	67	71.3
Foreign Language	82	58	70.7	92	45	48.9
Math	100	78	78.0	94	65	69.1
Science	96	69	71.9	94	66	70.2
Social Science	97	59	60.8	93	60	64.5
Business Education	72	44	61.1	92	63	68.5
All	549	388	70.7	559	366	65.5

Table 4

Teachers Providing Writing Samples

Subject	Number of Teachers	Percent Providing Samples
English	147	58.5
Foreign Language	103	25.2
Math	143	4.9
Science	135	28.9
Social Science	119	11.5
Business Education	107	15.9
Total	754	27.6

Table 5

Characteristics of Sampled Schools

Characteristics	Percent of Schools	
	Grade 9 n = 102	Grade 11 n = 94
Metropolitan status		
Metropolitan area	52.0	43.6
Urban fringe	19.6	22.3
Rural	28.4	34.0
Enrollment range		
Under 500	7.8	10.6
500–999	47.1	40.4
1000–2499	38.2	36.2
2500+	6.9	12.8
Region		
Northeast	20.6	27.7
North Central	29.4	24.5
South	28.4	37.2
West	21.6	10.6

Students	Averages	
Percent college bound	47.0	48.3
Percent nonwhite	11.9	10.4

Table 6

Characteristics of Sampled Classes and Teachers

Characteristics	Percent of Teachers Reporting								Chi-square tests	
	Subject Area						Grade			
	English	Foreign Language	Math	Science	Social Science	Business	Ninth	Eleventh	Subject	Grade
Class is:										
Required	72.3	3.0	15.5	23.9	75.2	5.7	43.7	24.9	442.98***	49.70***
Option in required area	21.3	4.0	50.7	28.4	14.2	9.5	27.1	20.6		
Elective	6.4	93.1	33.8	47.8	10.6	84.8	29.2	54.6	(df=10)	(df=2)
	(n=141)	(n=101)	(n=142)	(n=134)	(n=113)	(n=105)	(n=373)	(n=350)		
Ability:										
Mixed	32.1	35.6	20.3	25.4	45.5	40.2	34.3	30.1	86.47***	29.17***
Above average	28.6	51.6	47.6	46.3	18.8	18.7	27.9	43.0		
Average	26.4	12.9	23.1	19.4	25.9	38.3	25.5	23.2		
Below average	12.9	0.0	9.1	9.0	9.8	2.8	12.2	3.7	(df=15)	(df=3)
	(n=140)	(n=101)	(n=143)	(n=134)	(n=112)	(n=107)	(n=376)	(n=349)		
Teacher's age:										
Under 30	24.1	27.7	16.9	15.0	21.1	21.0	24.4	15.9	36.08*	11.14*
30–39	47.5	40.6	50.0	42.1	43.0	39.0	43.8	44.2		
40–49	14.2	10.9	22.5	24.1	24.6	28.6	19.1	22.5		
50–59	12.1	19.8	7.0	16.5	9.6	11.4	11.7	14.7		
60 or above	2.1	1.0	3.5	2.3	1.8	0.0	1.1	2.6	(df=20)	(df=4)
	(n=141)	(n=101)	(n=142)	(n=133)	(n=114)	(n=105)	(n=377)	(n=346)		

Procedures 23

| Characteristics | Percent of Teachers Reporting | | | | | | | | Chi-square tests | |
| | Subject Area | | | | | | Grade | | | |
	English	Foreign Language	Math	Science	Social Science	Business	Ninth	Eleventh	Subject	Grade
Teacher has supervisory responsibilities over other teachers	27.7 (n=141)	20.6 (n=102)	30.8 (n=143)	34.6 (n=133)	28.9 (n=114)	27.9 (n=104)	20.0 (n=375)	37.9 (n=348)	5.93 (df=5)	28.4*** (df=1)

| | Averages | | | | | | | | F-Statistics | | |
	English	Foreign Language	Math	Science	Social Science	Business	Ninth	Eleventh	Subject	Grade	Interaction
Class size	25.4 (n=119)	18.9 (n=80)	23.7 (n=122)	23.4 (n=101)	26.1 (n=86)	22.0 (n=86)	24.6 (n=306)	22.2 (n=288)	17.34** 5;582	25.20** 1;582	1.78 5;582
Years of teaching experience	12.8 (n=128)	11.7 (n=89)	13.3 (n=134)	14.5 (n=129)	12.1 (n=105)	12.2 (n=93)	11.82 (n=357)	14.11 (n=321)	2.18	16.32**	24.45

*p < .05; ** p < .01; *** p < .001

Substudies

In addition to the major observational and survey studies, several smaller-scale studies were undertaken to amplify the results. These involved (1) more intensive examination of episodes in which students wrote at least a paragraph, including observations of the behavior of selected pupils while they were writing; (2) interviews with students about their writing experiences and attitudes toward writing; and (3) interviews with selected teachers about instructional goals and teaching practices.

Writing Episodes and Student Writing Behavior

Within the broad spectrum of activities related to writing which can be observed in any secondary school classroom, a subset of activities involving continuous, original writing is of special interest. A relatively extensive coding system was developed to analyze these episodes, based on information recorded on the log of class activities (discussed above). An alternative observation system, focusing on the behavior of individual students during a writing episode, was also developed. Only thirty-three episodes were observed, however, and these usually included only prewriting activities or discussion of corrected work just returned by the teacher. This relatively low incidence of observed writing made the detailed coding and analysis irrelevant; observations drawn from the writing episodes that were observed will be dealt with anecdotally in the course of presenting and discussing other results.

Student Interviews

To add a third perspective to those provided by teacher responses and classroom observations, a standardized interview schedule taking between ten and forty-five minutes was prepared and piloted. Interviews with forty-one students (nominated by their English teachers as successful or unsuccessful ninth or eleventh grade writers) were completed; twenty-three were from the city high school and eighteen from the laboratory school. Each interview was tape recorded. Although portions of these interviews have been transcribed as illustrations of student responses, data were coded directly from the recordings. A copy of the final interview schedule (which asked about writing in a variety of subjects) is included in Applebee et al. (1980).

Teacher Interviews

Another substudy focused on the perceptions and classroom practices of eight city high school teachers selected to represent a range of subject areas and approaches. An interview schedule focusing on the types of writing they assign and the purposes of these assignments was prepared, and half-hour interviews were recorded with each teacher. These interviews were transcribed, and excerpts are used in the report that follows to help interpret the instructional emphases observed. A copy of the interview schedule used is included in Applebee et al. (1980).

Scoring Writing Samples

In both the observational studies and the national survey, samples of student writing in various subject areas were collected as illustrations of the kinds of writing tasks students were being asked to complete. After all data had been gathered, writing samples from both sources were compiled, edited to remove any identifying information (except code numbers), randomly ordered, and divided into six sets of approximately one hundred samples each. These sets of papers were then categorized by a team of six raters according to the implied audience for the writing and the function or purpose.

In both cases, one set of papers was put through the entire scoring process twice, with different raters or teams of raters, to obtain estimates of interrater agreement. The specific measures used are described at the appropriate points below in the presentation and discussion of results.

Analysis of Data

Project staff prepared data from all phases of this study for computer analysis. Analyses explored significant patterns of relationships among the various measures; given the design of the study, all such relationships are correlational rather than causal, though some of the relationships suggest causal hypotheses.

Dependent measures which approximated an equal-interval scale were analyzed using multivariate analysis of variance. Main and interaction effects were separately tested, using the classical model in which each effect is estimated after allowing for the influence of all other effects.

In these analyses, main effects of subject area, grade level, and teachers' attitudes were of much greater magnitude than were interaction effects (which for the most part were not statistically significant). This has allowed us to simplify the tables somewhat in presenting the results, presenting summary statistics separately by grade level and by subject area instead of displaying their full interaction. Similarly, chi-square analyses of nominal data concentrated on main effects and ignored interactions.

For some sets of variables, the two approaches were combined. Chi-square tests were used for individual items, partly because tables of percent-of-teachers-responding are simpler to interpret, and partly because this test makes few assumptions about the nature of the underlying scale. At the same time, multivariate analysis of variance was used for sets of related items to provide an overall test of the significance of each effect, given multiple measures on the same sample. Since the assumptions of an interval scale are rarely met in full in these analyses, the resulting test statistics should be treated as approximations rather than exact tests.

Summary

To investigate the nature and frequency of the writing tasks that secondary school students undertake, year-long observation of instruction in two contrasting secondary schools was combined with a national questionnaire survey of teachers in six major subject areas: English, mathematics, foreign language, science, social science, and business education. For the observational studies, observers used a simple log to record the activities in 259 lessons representing 13,293 minutes of instruction divided between ninth and eleventh grade classes in the two schools. Cooperation from the faculty in both schools was outstanding, with 85 percent of the teachers who might have participated allowing observers to visit on a random basis throughout the school year.

For the national survey, a two-stage sampling procedure was used. First, principals were asked to nominate a "good" teacher in each of the six target subject areas, and the nominated teachers were asked in turn to complete a questionnaire about writing and related activities in a specific class. In all, 83 percent of the principals and 68 percent of the teachers contacted provided useable responses, giving a national sample of 754 teachers stratified by school size and metropolitan status. The sample as a whole was skewed toward better teachers and classes; the teachers had more experience and more supervisory responsibilities than the typical teacher; and students of below average ability were underrepresented in the classes on which the teachers reported. The portrait of student writing that emerges from these responses might thus be expected to be a "best case" version of instruction in American schools.

3 The Writing Students Do

The first problem the research team confronted was how to describe the writing that students do. This problem had two parts: (1) where to draw the line between "writing" activities and other activities that might involve pencil and paper; and (2) given a range of writing activities (by whatever definition of writing), how to sort those activities into categories that would say something useful about the nature of the tasks that students were undertaking.

For research purposes, we decided to consider writing in the broadest possible sense as any activity in which students were using written language (including numbers) to record information or opinions for later reference by the teacher, fellow students, or themselves. In this sense, such activities as multiple-choice exercises, dictation, and translation were considered to be writing, even though these tasks involve supplying information rather than composing coherent text.

Uses of Writing

When it comes to describing the writing observed, previous work offers a variety of approaches, each appropriate for different purposes (see Cooper and Odell, 1977; Metzger, 1976; Tate, 1976 for overviews of major approaches). At the level of the text as a whole, the usual classification has been in terms of mode of discourse (narration, description, exposition, argumentation, and sometimes poetry). These modes have a long history and continue to be widely used in both experimental and descriptive studies (Donlan, 1974; Perron, 1977; Bereiter and Scardamalia, in press).

Though the modes are a convenient shorthand for describing certain techniques for organizing text passages, they ignore important dimensions involved in the use of language. Narrative, for example, can be used to support an argument, report information, or to tell a story; and its characteristics in each of these uses will vary in systematic ways (Kinneavy, 1971). James Britton (1970; et al., 1975), basing his work on a study of writing in the major subject areas of British schools, has proposed a comprehensive alternative to the traditional modes of discourse. As we saw in chapter 1, Britton's system is grounded in an analysis of the function (or use) of language represented by the writing sample.

The major categories within the system contrast language used to inform or persuade with that used to present an experience in a literary form. These distinctions have been used successfully in a number of recent studies by other investigators (Lunzer and Gardner, 1979; Renehan, 1977; Searle, 1975; Whale and Robinson, 1978). For the present study, Britton's terminology was re-worked to make it more useful for observational and self-report data. Also, it was extended to encompass a variety of tasks (all of which involve writing but not composing) that were not a concern in Britton's studies.

Figure 1 summarizes the categories. In the first set—writing without com-posing—all the tasks involve the use of written language, but in one way or another allow the student to bypass the problem of creating extended, coher-ent text. All tend to emphasize the accuracy of the specific information being supplied by the student, rather than the ability to organize and present that information coherently.

The second set—informational uses of writing—includes tasks that are what Britton et al. (1975) called *transactional* uses of language; they too share an emphasis on the use of writing to record or share information, but they differ from the mechanical writing tasks in that they all require the writer to shape the text, as well as to select and organize the information.

Within the general category of informational uses of writing there are three somewhat different types of activities represented. The first is note-taking, in which the demands for a well-shaped text are somewhat minimized. Though the notes may be very extensive, a variety of devices can be incorporated to abbreviate the text, including using outline form and special layout on the page. Ordinarily, the primary audience for the notes will be the writer and they do not need to be fully intelligible to anyone else.

Another type of activities within informational uses of writing is comprised of traditional essay and report writing tasks, here subdivided into a scale of increasing levels of abstraction (moving from *record* to *theory* in figure 1). Writing of this sort usually involves at least a paragraph, and it can range upward in length to extensive reports or, in out of school contexts, to full length books.

A final type of activity within informational uses of writing involves tasks in which the level of abstraction becomes less important than achieving a par-ticular effect on the reader. This is what Britton et al. (1975) call *conative* writing. It takes the form of writing in which (1) the attempt to convince overrides all other considerations (as in advertisements) or (2) rules are given in a context in which compliance is assumed (as in a list of school rules).

The third general set of writing activities in figure 1 involves personal uses of writing. Here the focus is on the interests and activities of the writer. Most typically, such writing takes the form of a journal or diary, or of letters or notes to close friends in which the main purpose is simply "keeping in touch." Some forms of note-taking can also fall into this category, particularly when the notes are used as a form of thinking-aloud on paper, a preliminary sorting out of new ideas or experiences. This is the type of writing that Britton et al. (1975) label *expressive.*

Writing without composing (mechanical uses of writing)
    Multiple-choice exercises.
    Fill-in-the-blank exercises (answered with less than a sentence).
    Short-answer exercises (brief, one or two sentences per question).
    Math calculations.
    Transcription from written material (copying).
    Transcription from oral sources (dictation).
    Translation.
    Other mechanical uses.
Informational uses of writing
    Note-taking.
    Record, of on-going experience. (This is what is happening.)
    Report. Retrospective account of particular events or series of events. (This is what happened.)
    Summary. Generalized narrative or description of a recurrent pattern of events or steps in a procedure. (This is what happens; this is the way it is done.)
    Analysis. Generalization and classification related to a situation, problem, or theme, with logical or hierarchical relationships among generalizations implicit or explicit.
    Theory. Building and defending at a theoretical level, including implicit or explicit recognition that there are alternative perspectives. Hypotheses and deductions from them.
    Persuasive or regulative uses of writing. (Any instances in which the attempt to convince overrides other functions or in which rules are given and compliance assumed.)
    Other informational uses.
Personal uses of writing
    Journal or diary writing, for own use.
    Personal letters or notes, where main purpose is "keeping in touch."
    Other personal uses.
Imaginative uses of writing
    Stories.
    Poems.
    Play scripts.
    Other imaginative uses.
Any other uses of writing

Figure 1. Uses of school writing.

The final set of writing activities in figure 1—imaginative uses of writing—shares an emphasis on the imaginative reconstruction of experience through stories, poems, or other literary art forms. Here the focus is on the nature of the particular experience rather than on the "information" conveyed. These are the types of writing which Britton et al. (1975) labelled *poetic,* to emphasize the role that the structure of the language itself plays in such writing.

In applying the categories from figure 1, writing in a foreign language was classified according to the kind of task being undertaken; "translation" was used only for direct translation from one language to another.

We should note, too, that the uses of writing summarized in figure 1 focus on school writing completed in class or at home. A broader study of writing unrelated to school might begin with the same major dimensions, but a variety of additional subcategories would be needed.

Each writing sample was scored by three raters working independently. Their assessments were then pooled; the verdict was based on agreement by at least two of the three raters. (Verdicts were possible in all cases.) Percent of agreement between two independent teams of three raters was .67 for a subsample of 82 papers (Holste, 1969). In the full sample, the individual raters averaged 69 percent agreement between their individual ratings and the final verdict. [The scoring manual used to apply these categories to school writing is included in Applebee et al. (1980).]

The Writing Observed

Using the broad definition of writing adopted for the purposes of the study, writing activities occupied a major proportion of class time in all of the subject areas observed. (See table 28, Appendix 1.) Pooling all observations, an average of 44 percent of the observed lesson time involved writing activities of one type or another. These activities were dominated by mechanical and informational uses of writing (occurring during an average of 24 and 20 percent of observed lesson time, respectively). Informational writing was dominated by note-taking (17 percent of observed time), however. On average, only 3 percent of lesson time was devoted to longer writing requiring the student to produce at least a paragraph of coherent text. Personal and creative uses of writing had little place in the high school curriculum, occupying less than one half of one percent of lesson time.

Homework assignments were similar. Of 118 assignments which we observed being given, only 3 percent asked for writing of at least paragraph length. The remainder were divided equally between "read and study" assignments and assignments calling for mechanical uses of writing.

Differences between schools and grade levels in the use of these activities were slight; they are summarized in full in table 28, Appendix 1. Subject-area differences were larger and are summarized in table 7.

Table 7

Mean Percent of Lesson Time Involving Writing Activities

Activity	Subject							Grade	
	English n=56	Foreign Language n=36	Math n=37	Science n=38	Social Science n=38	Business n=17	Other n=23	Ninth n=114	Eleventh n=145
Mechanical	16.1	15.4	47.6	25.4	12.3	31.5	10.4	25.1	22.8
Informational									
Note-taking	15.1	5.5	16.6	22.6	39.1	9.5	4.6	15.3	17.5
Other	8.3	0.5	0.0	0.0	5.1	2.0	0.0	3.7	2.3
Personal or Imaginative	1.6	0.1	0.0	0.0	0.0	0.0	0.0	0.0	0.8
Any Uses of Writing	41.1	21.5	64.2	48.1	56.4	43.0	15.0	44.1	43.3

Multivariate Analysis of Variance

Effect	Lambda	df	F-Statistic	Univariate F-Statistics			
				Mechanical	Informational		Personal or Imaginative
					Note-taking	Other	
School	.98	3;183	1.23	2.59	2.05	0.50	2.73
Grade	.98	3;183	1.05	0.49	2.07	1.39	2.33
Subject	.66	12;484	6.93***	8.69***	7.25***	4.49**	2.21
School X Grade	.98	3;183	1.30	1.31	1.62	0.36	2.71
School X Subject	.89	12;484	1.75*	1.49	2.43*	2.18	2.19
Grade X Subject	.89	12;484	1.89*	2.24	2.85*	1.20	2.35
School X Grade X Subject	.90	12;484	1.72	1.48	4.24**	0.36	2.15

$* p < .05; ** p < .01; *** p < .001$

In the academic subject areas, writing-related activities were used most in mathematics, science, and social science classes, and least in foreign language and English. In math, these activities primarily involved calculations; in science, they were usually short-answer (one or two sentence) responses to study sheets, often in the context of laboratory work. In grade eleven, the science classes involved a considerable proportion of calculations as well. Social science classes, particularly in the city high school, also made considerable use of short-answer, fill-in-the-blank, and multiple-choice exercises.

If we look instead at lesson time devoted to more extended writing (at least paragraph length), we find this occurred primarily in English classes (averaging 10 percent of lesson time); writing was also observed in social science classes, and to a lesser extent in foreign language, business education, and special education classes.

Note-taking also varied significantly with subject area. At one extreme, students in social science classes were observed taking notes some 39 percent of the time; at the other, students in foreign language classes took notes less than 6 percent of the time, and in special education classes they did not take them at all (table 28, Appendix 1). (These figures reflect class time when *any* student was taking notes.)

When asked about writing activities in their classes, students' descriptions paralleled observers' reports (table 8). Informational uses of writing, including note-taking, were by far the most prevalent tasks; imaginative uses were limited for the most part to English—and even there were reported by less than half of the students. (Personal uses of writing were not reported at all.) Interestingly, when asked a general question about the "writing" they did for their classes, well over a third of the students listed various sorts of mechanical writing activities as part of their responses. This suggests that the broad definition of writing adopted for the purposes of our research may be closer to an accepted use than we had originally thought. Teachers' comments occasionally left us with the same impression, as when we were told that a class was "full of writing" and discovered that what was meant was writing one-sentence answers to study questions. Similarly, we observed an "essay" test that asked the students to write "The Star Spangled Banner," and social science "writing" assignments that involved copying out whole sections of the text.

National Survey

Teachers completing the questionnaire for the national survey were asked to indicate the extent to which they made use of specific writing activities with the class on which they were reporting, for tests, class work, or homework. Each activity was rated as "not used with this class," "used occasionally," or "used frequently." Table 9 summarizes the results.

Table 8

Types of Writing Reported by Students

Type of Writing	Percent of Students Reporting					
	English n=42	Foreign Language n=31	Math n=39	Science n=32	Social Science n=32	Business Education n=13
Mechanical	19.0	32.3	76.9	31.3	31.3	53.8
Informational						
Note-taking	38.1	51.6	74.4	74.2[1]	75.0	53.8
Other	92.9	67.7	0.0	71.9	87.5	53.8
Imaginative	42.9	16.7[2]	0.0	0.0	0.0	7.7

1. n=31
2. n=30

As in the observational studies, teachers in all of the subject areas surveyed indicated that they made frequent use of at least some writing activities, taking writing in the broad sense. These activities were dominated by note-taking and short-answer responses (requiring at most a few sentences per question), however; paragraph-length writing was reported as a frequent activity for only 27 percent of the classes at grade nine, and 36 percent at grade eleven. English, by a very wide margin, was most likely to require such writing; mathematics, least likely. The use of all seven activities sampled differed significantly among the six subject areas. Activities requiring only short-answer responses tended to be used less frequently, and paragraph length writing more frequently, in grade eleven than in grade nine. Mathematical calculations and proofs also increased between grades nine and eleven, in part because of their increasing use in science as well as mathematics classes at the upper grades.

The six subject areas studied differ not only in the extent to which they make use of writing of at least paragraph length, but also in the type of writing they assign when they do make such assignments. Tables 10 and 11 summarize the relevant results, both from teacher reports and from the writing samples that they supplied. (Since teachers were asked to supply two samples, separate tests of grade and subject differences were calculated for the "good" and the "poor" papers.)

The categories *record* through *theory* in figure 1 represent a scale of levels of abstraction. The record of ongoing experience is at the lowest end of the scale; it involves a relatively direct recoding from experience into words—the kind of following-the-action that occurs, for example, in a radio broadcast of a sporting event. This is a relatively rare form in writing and was not included in the categories on the teacher questionnaire. As expected, less than 1 percent of the writing samples fell into this category. The following example is typical of such writing in its present tense presentation and moment-by-moment narrative organization:

> Suddenly the top of the tree starts to break up and fall. The guy is terrified and very confused. The top of the tree is swaying wildly like a kite in the wind. It's meraculous that it hasn't fallen yet. He is despertly tring to get down but the tree is like a pendulum on a clock. Finally he is descending. The tree grabs him and pins him 30 feet in the air. He staggers to his feet almost falling on to the ground below. He gathers a little strength and begins chopping some branches off. He climbs down on the stubs of the branches. The ground welcomes him as he reaches it. (ninth grade English)

The report on particular events also remains quite close to immediate experience, though it is recalled experience retrospectively described. This was used most frequently by the science teachers who assign writing; it was cited in frequent use by 30 percent of the social science and 24 percent of the English teachers as well. In the writing samples, report occurred about 20 percent of the time and was used fairly evenly by the various subject areas.

Table 9

Use of Writing-Related Activities

| | Percent of Teachers Reporting Frequent Use | | | | | | | | Chi-square tests[1] | |
| | Subject Area | | | | | | Grade | | | |
Activity	English n=142	Foreign Language n=103	Math n=143	Science n=135	Social Science n=113	Business n=107	Ninth n=378	Eleventh n=352	Subject df=10	Grade df=2
Multiple-choice or fill-in-the-blank	22.5	24.3	9.1	51.1	55.8	32.7	31.2	32.4	122.00***	0.99
Note-taking	51.4	37.9	49.0	68.9	67.3	28.0	49.5	54.8	68.88***	3.42
Copying, dictation, or translation	12.0	70.9	18.2	20.7	14.2	35.5	28.0	24.1	153.00***	1.50
Calculations	2.8	1.0	99.3	43.7	2.7	47.7	29.9	40.6	587.30***	17.61***
Short-answer	50.0	65.0	16.8	55.6	51.8[2]	29.9	48.5[3]	39.8	122.80***	7.70*
Proofs	4.2	0.0	38.5	17.8	1.8[2]	19.6	8.7[3]	20.7	263.02***	21.31***
Paragraph-length writing	82.4	26.2	1.4	14.8	36.3	15.9	26.5	35.5	436.00***	7.04*

Multivariate Analysis of Variance

Effect	Lambda	df	F-Statistic
Subject	0.14	35; 2964	50.26***
Grade	0.94	7; 704	6.02****
Interaction	0.83	35; 2964	3.76***

1. Chi-square tests are based on three-point scales: not used, used occasionally, used frequently.
2. n=114 3. n=379
* p < .05; ** p < .01; *** p < .001

Table 10

Types of Writing Reported by Teachers Who Assign Writing of
at Least Paragraph Length

| Type of Writing | Percent of Teachers Reporting Frequent Use | | | | | | | | Chi-square tests[1] | |
| | Subject Area | | | | | | Grade | | | |
	English n=139	Foreign Language n=65	Math n=19	Science n=84	Social Science n=95	Business n=49	Ninth n=215	Eleventh n=227	Subject df=10	Grade df=2
Informational										
Report	24.0	7.7	0.0	35.6	29.8	2.9	20.9	26.0	113.37***	2.71
Summary	12.2	9.2	15.8	44.0	20.0	12.2	16.3	23.3	89.71***	4.73
Analysis	41.7	6.2	15.8	42.9	49.5	14.3	30.7	39.2	117.50***	3.51
Theory	20.9	3.1	52.6	41.7	16.8	6.1	14.0	29.1	119.12***	16.54***
Personal	25.9	18.5	0.0	7.1	3.2	18.4	14.0	15.4	99.34***	1.02
Imaginative	34.5	21.5	0.0	0.0	1.1	2.0	14.4	13.2	178.14***	2.93
Other	11.5	15.4	0.0	6.0	1.1	20.4	8.8	9.3	41.72***	0.10

Multivariate Analysis of Variance

Effect	Lambda	df	F-Statistic
Subject	0.31	35; 1761	16.31***
Grade	0.92	7; 418	4.98***
Interaction	0.88	35; 1761	1.54*

1. Chi-square tests are based on three-point scales: not used, used occasionally, used frequently.

$*p < .05; **p < .01; ***p < .001$

Table 11

Writing Samples: Types of Writing Represented

| | Percent of Papers | | | | | |
| | Subject Area | | | | Grade | |
Types of Writing	English n=182	Science n=70	Social Science n=67	Business n=24	Ninth n=182	Eleventh n=167
Informational						
Record	1.0	0.0	1.5	0.0	1.6	0.0
Report	19.2	15.7	17.9	37.5	22.5	17.4
Summary	13.2	47.1	22.4	16.7	25.8	18.6
Analysis	39.0	32.9	44.8	33.3	31.9	45.5
Theory	2.2	2.9	4.5	0.0	1.6	4.2
Persuasive	0.5	0.0	3.0	4.2	1.1	1.2
Personal	8.8	1.4	6.0	8.3	7.1	6.0
Imaginative						
Stories	12.1	0.0	0.0	0.0	6.0	5.4
Poems	3.8	0.0	0.0	0.0	2.2	1.8

Chi-square (subject area), df=12, good papers=42.99, p < .001, poor papers=25.35, p < .01. (For the chi-square tests, related function categories were collapsed to raise expected frequencies.)

Chi-square (grade), df=5, good papers=5.89, p < .21, poor papers=6.89, p < .14

The following samples illustrate some of the ways reporting tasks were used in different subject areas:

The Hunch Back of Notre Dame

The story begins on the side steps of the Notre Dame Cathedral in Paris in the year fourteen hundred and forty-eight years six month and nineteen day. That historic day that the boy Quasimodo or Hunchback or to the religious people Beelezebub was found by the Monk Claude Frollo.

After caring for Quasimodo in his own room Claude Frollo made him a room in the cellar of the cathedral. Though he was an extremely ugly creature Claude Frollo was very fond of him and he was a great source of joy to him. You see Quasimodo was born this way: he had a tetrahedron nose, horse-shoe mouth, a little left eye stubbled up with an eyebrow of carroty bristles, while the right eye was completely overwhelmed and buried by an enormous wen. He had jagged teeth like an elephant which were covered by a horny lip. He had a fork chin, & his head was covered with a kind of red bristels. Between his shoulders rose an enormous hump, which was counter-balanced by a protuberance in front. His thighs and legs were so strangely put together that they touched at no one point but the knees. His feet were immense, his hands monstrous . . . .

Realizing what he had done and the futility of it all, Quasimodo wiped one last tear from his tear-stained eye and departed from the bell-tower by jumping off. (ninth grade French)

What I Saw at the Nuclear Reactor

At the Nuclear Reactor, I saw a lot of things that looked very unusual to me. I got to use the machine that shows if you have been exposed to radiation. Our tour guide took us to the room that contained the reactor. It was really neat. The reactor had blue water in the top. Then we went downstairs where we saw a window like place. Inside was a robot arm that you could control. The robot arm is used from the outside of the window for handling radioactive materials that is too dangerous for humans to handle. Our tour guide had on a film badge on his shirt, finger-n-wrist. Our tour guide told us that police could bring them hair from a person, who might have committed a crime and the people at the nuclear reactor could tell the police who the person was. Its like the procedure used for fingerprints. (ninth grade Science)

A White Ball of Fur

About a month ago, my mama brought home a little ball of fur. It's name is Pete and he cost a hundred and twenty-five dollars. He's so cute. He's got little brown eyes and soft white fur. He is so mean though. He tears up our slippers and shoes, and he nips at our heels when we walk. He's also very smart, he can open doors and climb shelves and he can get on the sofa. Pete's very curious, he like to play with the basketball, so when he see's a basketball game on T.V., he tries to get the basketball. He also wants to get that cat on the Good Mews commercial. (ninth grade English)

The first two of these examples are very typical of writing at the level of report. Like the record of ongoing experience, they rely heavily on narrative sequence for their organization, but they shift to the past tense and recount far less of the moment-by-moment detail. The third writing sample, "A White Ball of Fur," begins to shift from a report about the specific tricks of a new puppy toward a summary of the puppy's characteristics—"he nips at our heels" and "he can open doors."

Summary, based on a pattern of recurring events, represents a step up in the level of abstraction; here the writer generalizes from particular events in order to draw conclusions about "how Pete behaves . . .," "what happens when . . .," or "how one goes about . . . ." These generalizations remain very close to the experiences in which they are based, however, and usually continue to rely on narrative sequence for their structure and organization. On the questionnaire, science and social science teachers were most likely to make frequent use of assignments of this sort. When the writing samples that they supplied were classified according to type, summary represented just over a fifth of the writing in the social sciences, and nearly half of that from science classes. Typically, a summary described steps in a process or procedure, as in the following examples:

> *Describe how an unstable atomic nucleus becomes stable.*
>
> When the isotope is radioactive, one of the nuclei throws an alpha particle. This then decreases both atomic mass & number. Then if the next element formed is also radioactive and may give off a beta particle which then causes an increase in the atomic number. This process continues until a stable element is formed. (ninth grade Earth Science)

> *Explain the technique used to separate two compounds by chromatography.*
>
> You have two liquids and must heat them sufficiently to boil the lower liquid's point. The liquid turns to vapor and you have some type of tube system that takes the vapors to a new chamber to condense, then boil them, as you do this over and over your amount of liquid grows smaller, and so does your increase in % of gain. This is why pure substances are so expensive. (twelfth grade Chemistry)

> Building a window frame can be a hard job. The first step in building a window frame is getting the right supplies. Wood and nails are the two supplies needed. First you cut out the wood. Then you take the pieces and put them in the order they should be put together. When getting pieces of wood in order take small finishing

nails and nail frame together. Finally get piece of glass and slide in frame and make secure and your job is through. (ninth grade English)

To solve one type of quadratic equation you must first simplify both sides. After this is done get all of the terms on one side. The next step is to factor and set each answer to "x". Another type of quadratic equation is one that cannot be factored. A formula $(x = -b + b2 - 4ac)$ is used to solve this. The value before the "x2" *and* its sign become *a,* and the value before the "x" and it's sign become *b,* and the last value and its sign become *c.* Next, you plug a, b, and c into the problem and solve it as usual. (ninth grade Algebra)

It is typical of such summaries that they read very authoritatively; this *is* the way it is to be done. It is also typical that they make little attempt to explain *why* a particular set of steps or procedures is effective; there is little explanation of the underlying processes or motivation.

When the writer attempts to explain these processes, the writing moves toward analysis, the next level of abstraction. Analysis involves classification and categorization of the phenomenon being examined, making use of hierarchical relationships and logical connections among generalizations to explain what is happening. Writing of this sort was the most frequent type of school writing, both in teacher reports and in the samples they supplied. It was less likely to be reported in frequent use among the business education, mathematics, and foreign language teachers. The following examples illustrate the sorts of tasks being undertaken:

The reason I think summer is hear is that I see the birds nesting and all the baby animals are out anouther reason is that it is getting warm out and the lakes are warming up and all the trees bushes and grass is turning green. Plus I know summer is hear because of the thunderstorms and bad weather that is being thrown at us. but on nice day all the people go to the beach and to lake michigan to get a tan. all the fruits are becoming ripe and need picking and the farmers are bailing hay so that young people can get a job. (eleventh grade English)

1. a. Generally, as the temperature increases so does the reaction. This situation was observed when magnesium ribbon was placed in three different temperatures of water. The hotter the water, the more quickly the magnesium reacted. (eleventh grade Chemistry)

Martin Eden
Martin's individual success was empty and lacking in conviction because he really wasn't accomplishing anything for himself. Instead he did it all for the woman he loved. However, some of his accomplishments were for personal gain.

The girl Martin Eden was in love with was rather wealthy and also a college graduate. Martin, on the other hand, had very little education and was rather a poor sailor.

After Martin met her, he immediately became infactuated with her. He also realized that if he was going to get anywhere with her he would have to change and change drastically.

He started taking baths and stopped drinking. He also started to read alot of literature and also started to write. He even rented a typewriter.

Martin was soon able to talk the way she talked which was also a goal he had set for himself.

In time both Ruth and Martin fell in love with each other. However, it didn't last long. Ruth's parents stoped it very quickly because they didn't feel Martin was worthy of their daughter.

Martin only became more determined after his rejection. He soon became a highly respected and well-paid author. Ruth found this out and went back to him but only for his money. Martin soon found this out and killed himself. However, he did not kill himself just because of Ruth. He had other problems also. One of Martin's other problems was his struggle against the bourgeois society.

As you can see Martin's main reason for living was Ruth, and when he lost her, he couldn't handle it. Anybody with conviction and dedication to his proffession would have been able to handle the situation better than Martin did. (ninth grade English)

Conspiracy

Conspiracy: an agreement between 2 or more people or parties to commit an unlawful or to accomplish a lawful end by unlawful means. There are many reasons this would be done. Although we know little about the Pontiac Conspiracy, we know that he, a great indian, conspired with other indian tribes to prevent U.S. Army attack. I really don't see why this is a conspiracy because it was all for lawful means. Assasination of a President you would figure to be a conspiracy also. The assasination of Lincoln was a conspiracy also. The assasination of Garfield wasn't because the assasin, Guiteau, didn't conspire with anyone. He shot the president because he was refused an office spot in Washington and to help things along he was insane. Alger Hiss vs. Whittaker Chambers case was a conspiracy. Alger Hiss was accoused by Chambers of giving confidential material to USSR. Although accoused and proven guilty to this date Hiss still states he is inocent. The Kennedy assination really can't be said if or not it was a conspiracy. Some people say only one person shot at and hit Kennedy but some say one of two people shot.

In eather case it could or couldn't be a conspiracy. Watergate was a conspiracy. The Republicans had the phones taped so they could gain in the upcoming election. Arron Burr was a conspiracy. It seems he was conspiring against the government. He wanted to take over the land West of the Appl. Mts. To do this he needed an army so he conspired with the British government. His plans were shot when his close associate told on him.

All of the above examples show examples of conspiracy. Wheather or not proven guilty or not considered a conspiracy all these acts were acts against the government or government official. (eleventh grade American History)

Theorizing in a systematic way, including making hypotheses and drawing deductions from them, represented the highest level of abstraction in the various types of writing. Although a substantial proportion of the teachers reported "frequently" asking students to write at this level of abstraction, the writing that resulted rarely moved beyond analysis. Only 3 percent of the samples were categorized as theorizing. The speculations about the future embedded in the following paper represent one kind of writing that falls into this category:

"Go West, young man, go West"; such was the cry encouraging ambitious Americans to forge westward in search of exciting prosperity. Our society today regards the pioneers as heroes because of their brave spirit, yet many people have no conception of the hardships they faced and the obstacles they overcame.

I had the privilege to experience some of the escapades of a pioneer when my American History class (after six months of preparation), went on a six-day wagon trek across the desert. I acquired an immense admiration and appreciation for those courageous Americans who crossed the plains in covered wagons. My wonderment of the pioneers and the life they led was interrupted by my curiosity of how future generations would relate to the people of the present era. Perhaps a century from now, a history class studying the current period would take a "car caravan" across the country in order to better understand our way of life.

Wagon Travel involved many perils and risks. Indians were a major problem, along with rugged virgin trails and the complications with beasts of burden. Today's mode of transportation seems unchallenging when compared with that of the pioneers. Twenty-first century travel may view our highway travel as dangerous because of such factors as engine failure and human error in driving. Space-age travel will be somewhat devoid of hazardous venture because of machine-regulated safety.

By 2080, cars will be obsolete, and the distance "from sea to shining sea" will be considered a mere excursion. Highly technological spacecraft will replace our automobiles, just as horse and wagon were superceded by motor vehicles. For the entirety of our travels, we existed (quite comfortably) without modern conveniences including watches, radios, and televisions. Students embarking on an auto expedition a hundred years from now might find they must leave behind their pocket computers or other devices from a Ray Bradbury story. Technology is an important factor when contrasting the present with the past and future.

The greatest enrichment of this trip was the harmony which I felt with nature. Out there in the desert, distant from any form of civilization, one is better able to understand Thoreau's philosophy of natural simplicity. Future generations living in the next century may have no contact with planetary nature. A green patch of grass in the median of a highway may be the only touch with nature space age citizens might have. This small piece of the earth in its original state may be inspiring to future citizens just as I was engulfed in the beauty of the mountains and the desert. What a shame that this may be the outcome of technological society!

The wagon trip was a great learning experience due to the athenticity of the project. I was prompted to contemplate the comparisons between the three different epochs in the areas of the courageous spirit, technology and nature. My inquisitiveness remains about how my great-great-grandchildren will view the history of my generation. Most importantly, I discovered that in order to understand better the world of the present, one must consider both the past and the future. (eleventh grade American History)

A more formal use of hypotheses and deductions from them is evident in the excerpts below, drawn from a sixteen-page typewritten report:

I have 3 generations of cats which will be the basis of my problem. I am attempting to determine how the F1 and F2 generations inherited their coat colors and also determine the parents' phenotypes and genotypes. I am dealing with dominant and recessive genes, genes that are neither dominant or recessive to each other, and sex-linked genes.

My hypotheses were that the yellow tabby tom cat was the father of the first litter of the F1 generation, and the F2 generation; and that the grey tabby tom cat was the father of the 2nd and 3rd litters of the F1 generation. My research has shown that by the way the genes were inherited, these most likely were the correct fathers . . . .

Summary

The gene for Orange is sex-linked and is carried on the X chromosome. An orange male crossed with a non-orange female. The results were tortoiseshell females and a non-orange male. Males can only receive either a dominant gene or a recessive, not both. That is why there are no tortoiseshell because it takes both to make a tortoiseshell.

This same male then crosses with one of its tortoiseshell daughters. The results were one orange male and one tortoiseshell female.

This male was also a tabby. Veet was a non-tabby. The results were 3 non-tabbies and one hybrid tabby. They didn't come out the way they were supposed to but it could've been because of certain reasons.

Again this male also crossed with his daughter-a non-tabby. Their offspring were one hybrid tabby and one non-tabby and these were the way they were supposed to be.

Tabby and black are neither dominant or recessive to each other. A hybrid black female crossed with a hybrid tabby male. The results are 3 hybrid tabbies and 2 hybrid blacks. Whether you are comparing tabby to non-tabby or black to non-black, the offspring were pretty close to what they should be.

In this study I did prove my hypotheses that Tom, the yellow tabby was the father of the first litter of the F1 and the F2; and that the grey tabby was the father of the 2nd and 3rd litters of the F1 generation . . . . (eleventh grade Biology)

Persuasive writing, where the attempt to sell a particular point of view overrides all other concerns, was not included as a separate item on the teacher questionnaire, and represented only about 1 percent of the writing in the samples teachers supplied. One form in which it appears in school work is in mock advertisements; another is in political contexts, as in the following paper:

The Change in Economy

Another election year is here, and Carter is taking the honors. But why? Because of the Iranian situation or because he has helped our economy over the past 4 years.

Well, maybe the change in the economy is so slow that we don't realize how downhill things are going.

In the past Carter term this is how things have gone down hill: the cost of living is up 31%, and the people's incomes are only up 7.3%.

The dollar's value has gone down 18.7% and who are getting these profits: the corporations. Their profits are up 63.1%!

Well, Carter hasn't been all bad the unemployment is down 23.4%. But should Carter get the credit for it. And should Carter get the blame for our economic position? Well, maybe if Carter gets out of office then we'll see what the other man can do. (ninth grade Business Education)

Personal and imaginative writing, though popular among English and foreign language teachers, were rarely reported in frequent use in other subject areas. This was borne out in the writing samples, where informational writing represented 85 percent of the sample and all other types of writing 15 percent. Even in English classes, only about a quarter of the writing samples represented personal or imaginative uses of language.

When personal writing did occur, it sometimes took the form of "friendly letters" to relatives or classmates—albeit sometimes in artificial contexts. An assignment on "The Value of a Yearbook" produced one such piece:

Laramy, Wyoming 50213
September 25, 1980

Dear Vicky,

Howdy! How's life up in the Alaskan boonies? It's just beautiful here in Wyoming. The sun shines every day and the nights are cool and calm. It's really a much more beautiful state than I ever would have imagined.

You know, I really miss all my friends up there. Are they all changing? Boy I'm glad I bought a yearbook! At first I thought it was just a fad. I thought people only bought them to be "in" To be perfectly honest, that's why I bought mine! But now, as I look back at the faces and the names, I can remember all the fun times I had at service.

I almost didn't buy a yearbook because I thought, "Well, I'm just a freshman. It's really not too important. I mean, I'll be here for three more years." But my views about that changed when I found out we were moving to Wyoming.

When I first moved here I would look through my yearbook at the pictures and the things people wrote to me and I would have a "sob session." But now I realize that it's good to remember people and the influence they had on my life. I should remember what I liked in them and try to develop those characteristics in myself. Yes, my yearbook has really become one of my most dearly treasured possessions.

I guess I'd best close now; it's getting late. Say "Hi" to Laur, Whit, and Susan for me. And *please* write back soon.

Love,
Becky
(ninth grade English)

Personal writing also occurs at times in "loosening up" exercises, which can be used either to get students around the fear of writing at all or as raw material out of which more polished material can later be shaped:

I'm thinking about how stupid these people act when ask to do something and I think it is dumb because they talk about everything epesically Cariloyn, Becky & Tammy. Shhhhh!!!! I can't concentrate.

10 min sure is a long time I wonder if it is over yet, I doubt it because I still wound'nt be writing if the 10 min. was up, so I guess it is not up so I will keep on writing till I'm trough.

I'm thinking about what I'm am going to do tonight like (go out and drink refer and smoke beer).

I'm thinking about our new house that we are going to move into tonight on Jan. 25. I like the house because it is sharp.

What I am doing now is not usually because I have to write speeches all the time for drama class, I have been in it for 3 years.

I wish I were at home with a coke and some sort of a snack and watching t.v.

This is all right writing about what you are doing. I just thinging about what Becky said "Dennis you creep."

I'm thinking about how much longer I have to write which is about 1 min. I don't know what else to write except that this class is about to end and I hope Bill Sorrells has brought that paper

I need for single living and if he didn't I think I'll cuss him out
and then cut his head and then pull his toes off and cut his legs
off and then I might get mad. (eleventh grade English)

Although the use of all of the types of writing investigated differed significantly between subject areas, only theorizing showed significant grade level
differences; the percent of teachers claiming to assign such writing *frequently*
rose from 14 to 29 percent between grades nine and eleven. With the writing
samples supplied by the teachers, the overall effect of grade level on type of
writing was not significant for either the better papers or the poorer ones.
Considering just the categories *record* through *theory*, however, a significantly
higher proportion of grade eleven than grade nine papers were categorized
as analysis or theory ($p < .02$ for both the better and the poorer papers).
Together with the teachers' reports, this suggests that the level of abstraction
of informational writing increases in the upper grades.

Since teachers were asked to select papers representing either the top quarter
or bottom quarter of those produced in response to a particular assignment, it
was also possible to examine the relationship between student ability and the
type of writing produced. Here there was a tendency for those papers chosen
as better by the teachers to involve analysis or theorizing (49.3 percent, compared with 34.4 percent of those selected as poorer writing). (Considering just
the categories *record* through *theory*, the better papers were significantly more
likely to involve analysis or theorizing, chi-square for correlated proportions =
8.8, df = 1, $p < .01$.)

Audiences for Student Work

Every piece of writing is shaped not only by its function (or use), but also
by a conception of the audience to whom it is addressed (Mead, 1934; Eco,
1979). Audience affects virtually every aspect of language use, including syntax,
diction, length, level of abstraction, and method of organization (Bracewell,
Scardamelia, and Bereiter, 1978; Crowhurst and Piche, 1979; Rubin and Piche,
1979).

In the present study, audiences for student writing were categorized simply:
no clear audience; only the writer (as in private diary writing); the teacher,
to grade or assess the work; the teacher, as part of an ongoing instructional
dialogue; and wider audience, known or unknown. Again, this is an adaptation
of a set of audience categories proposed by Britton, et al. (1975), simplified
for our purposes.

As with function, each writing sample was scored for audience by three
raters working independently, and a "verdict" was based on agreement by at
least two out of three. Interrater reliability estimated as percent of agreement

between two independent teams of raters was .71 for a subsample of 82 papers. In the sample as a whole, the individual raters averaged 77 percent agreement between their individual ratings and the final verdict.

Analysis of audiences for student writing focused on writing of at least paragraph length. In the thirty-three writing episodes that were seen in the observational studies, the audience was clearly the teacher, with the expectation that the work would be graded and evaluated. Too few writing episodes were observed to draw useful conclusions about similarities or differences between grade levels or subject areas.

The questionnaire used in the national survey had a list of people who might read student writing, each to be rated as "never," "sometimes," or "regularly" reading writing from the class. Table 12 summarizes the results for teachers who regularly used writing of at least paragraph length for homework, class-work, or tests of progress. (Teachers who assigned writing only on the final exam were instructed to skip this section of the questionnaire.)

Clearly, the teacher in the role of judge or examiner is the prime audience for student writing, in all subject areas. Fewer than 10 percent of the teachers reported that student writing was regularly read by other students; even in English classes, only 16 percent of the teachers reported such audiences. A slightly higher proportion reported some use of writing that was read only by the student; such uses were concentrated in mathematics, science, and social science classes. The vast majority of teachers reported that they regularly read student work both to assign a grade and make other comments.

The writing samples supplied by many of the teachers show the same overall pattern (table 13). Fully 88 percent of the samples were categorized by our raters as addressed to the teacher as the primary audience; only a third were written as part of a teaching-learning dialogue, rather than as a display of completed learning. (None of the samples had the writer as his or her own primary audience, but that was to be expected in a context where the teacher is providing samples of students' work.)

Writing as part of a teacher-learner dialogue (where the student could expect a response to ideas in progress of development rather than evaluation of completed learning) was more likely in English and the social sciences than in science or business education. When it did occur, it often centered on personal experiences or opinions that cannot easily be treated as tests of content-area learning (though such writing can be given as a test of writing skills). The following examples, both from English classes, are typical:

New Outlooks

The first thing I think about when I look back on my younger years in Grand Forks is the summertime fragrances of our back-yard apple trees in bloom. My girlfriend, Erica, and I used to spend all of the heated, humid days in the shade of the big apple tree in

Table 12

Audiences Regularly Provided for Student Writing by Teachers
Who Assign Writing of at Least Paragraph Length

Audience	Percent of Teachers Reporting								Chi-square test[1]	
	Subject Area						Grade			
	English n=140	Foreign Language n=70	Math n=17	Science n=89	Social Science n=100	Business n=57	Ninth n=224	Eleventh n=237	Subject df=10	Grade df=2
Only the student	7.1	7.1	23.5	18.0	17.0	8.8	8.9	14.3	22.07*	3.27
Teacher, to react without assigning grade	15.0	8.6	17.6	4.5	9.0	22.8	14.3	10.1	24.68**	2.86
Teacher, to grade without other comment	6.4	12.9	11.8	16.9	15.0	12.3	12.1	12.2	26.75***	0.45
Teacher, to react and grade	77.1	68.6	44.4[2]	80.9	75.0	68.4	72.0[3]	76.4	18.53*	1.43
Other students	16.4	7.1	5.9	1.1	3.0	5.3	5.8	9.7	58.75***	8.6*
Other	3.6	5.7	0.0	2.2	1.0	5.3	4.5	1.7	15.99	4.13

Multivariate Analysis of Variance

Effect	Lambda	df	F-Statistic
Subject	.76	30;1758	4.13***
Grade	.99	6;439	1.09
Interaction	.95	30;1758	0.81

1. Chi-square tests are based on three-point scales: never, sometimes, regularly. 2. n=18 3. n=225

* $p < .05$; ** $p < .01$; *** $p < .001$

Table 13

Writing Samples: Audience Addressed

Audience	Percent of Papers						
	Subject Area				Grade		
	English n=182	Science n=69	Social Science n=67	Business n=22	Ninth n=181	Eleventh n=164	
Teacher, as part of teacher-learner dialogue	42.9	15.9	35.8	4.5	33.7	33.5	
Teacher, as examiner	47.8	66.7	58.2	54.5	56.4	52.4	
Wider audience, known or unknown	9.3	17.4	6.0	40.9	9.9	14.0	

Chi-square (subject area), df=6: Good papers=16.18, $p < .01$; Poor papers=39.44, $p < .001$
Chi-square (grade), df=2: Good papers=0.31, nsd; Poor papers=0.04, nsd

my backyard. The life moves so much slower here. I never really appreciated the slower-moving ways of the people who live in my hometown of Grand Forks, ND until I went away one summer for a month to San Francisco, California. The excitement there is chilling in a way, and no one *really* knows anyone else. You're kind of a number. When my plane landed back in Grand Forks, I wasn't *glad* to be home because I've always hated going "home," but I was relieved, in a way. This town felt very reassuring in many ways. I remember how all the memories of those backyard-summer days and the Saturday afternoon shopping sprees downtown came flooding back to me. I laughed a little to myself as I think back on how much trouble Erica and I got in when we got caught playing on the bike trails in Lincoln Park by the river. We had such a good time catching butterflies down in the weedy patches by the river shore and daring each other to go in the water even though we both knew how dangerous and deceiving that twisting, churning undercurrent of the Red River of the North was. The good times by that river were endless until the day we got caught by my dad and each of us got grounded for a week!! I've never seen my father so upset!

He's gone now—the good times are gone too, mostly, but what remains in my memory will never go away. (eleventh grade English)

This Class

Some of the kids in the class are craze but I don't think I could make it threw the day without them. They make you laugh even when your down and they seem to make the day go fast.

I think I've learn a lot in this class even if I can't do all the work but I try and that what I think counts.

I like to do these writing assiments because I even like to now what I'm going to write about and have to say about it. Class have there ups and down and I think most of are up because of the thing we do like the books we read the assiments we have. (eleventh grade English)

Sometimes students move into a teacher-learner dialogue even when faced with an assignment which is designed to test their knowledge of a topic. Something of the sort happens in the following example, which begins as a test of whether the student has read *Future Shock* and understood the concepts of "serial marriage" and "marriage trajectory," but moves on to explore some more personal reactions:

According to Alvin Toffler, "until death do us part" will soon become non-existent. With the accelerated rate of change in society, the conventional marriage bears very little chance of being successful. People will become "more frenzied" in their search for love and therefore get married. As their life progresses, and goes through the various stages, their expectations and what they want from a marriage changes. This is where according to Toffler, serial marriages come in. These are successive temporary marriages which can be left behind at the individual's wishes. In *Future Shock,* Toffler indicates that these serial marriages are already in effect. Cohabitation is considered in this category because it is actually a sort of probationary marriage. This will be one of several stages of the marriage career or trajectory. The trajectory will include several critical points where a change in lifestyle is made. Serial marriages are not the only solution, according to the book. Careers can be the primary concern, with marriage taking place after retirement. Perhaps this will increase the chances of "until death do us part" actually happening.

I don't believe any of these things will happen at least not to such an extreme. Succesive marriages do occur through divorce and remarriage, but as yet, they are still not fully accepted as the norm. I believe that if there is any change in the institution of marriage, it will be for the better. As society changes people will look for one individual to center their life around. Their spouse will become a sort of security blanket, and this will help couples appreciate each other more. (eleventh grade Social Science)

Over half of the samples seemed directed to the teacher as examiner. One of the paradoxes involved in such writing is that writing for this audience requires less writing skill than virtually any other audience. Because teachers know what information they are looking for, they can make the transitions and connections necessary to make the writing coherent; they can read what the student "meant to say"—but in fact did not. Sarah, one of the eleventh graders interviewed, pointed out how oddly formed writing to the teacher-as-examiner may sometimes be. Talking about a social studies test, she says:

Normally it will be a compare essay where we're supposed to compare two periods with several different things. I don't write an introduction to these, 'cause I rarely have the time. So I'll just go in and I'll show the differences in very short paragraphs. For everything, for every topic that he gave us, I'll show the differences and if I have time I'll add a little conclusion at the end which will tell what I really think.

A science teacher at the same school explained that such an approach matches teachers' expectations: "If they get the content, and it's organized, I know what they are trying to say, then they get their credit." The following samples show something of the range of writing that occurs in this category.

But for every enemy that these acts made for the President in Wall Street or in the business lobbies at Washington, he was described as carrying a big stick and was named the trust buster. (eleventh grade American History)

He graduated from Harvard in 1880, and then spent 2 years on a ranch in North Dakota to build up his health. He served in the N.Y. State legislature, on the National Civil Service Commission,

and as president of the police board in N.T.C. In 1897, he was
appointed to Assistant Secretary of the Navy. He soon resigned,
however, to help organize the "Rough Riders" in the Spanish war.
He was elected governor of N.Y. (1898), Vice President (1900) and
he bacame president upon McKinley's death (1901). (eleventh
grade American History)

*Discuss the irony in "Solo on the Drums," giving specific illustra-
tions.*
The irony in Solo on the Drums is that the drummer is a famous
guy and most famous guys have girls hanging on him.
    Another ironic thing is the a member of the band, a Marquis
of Brund, has taken his girl away from him. In a way it seems he
still respects the guy because he talks of how he plays such a sweet
piano. (eleventh grade English)

The Yankee's previous opinion of the king was that he was no
more than a lummox. He held this thought until in the poxhouse
the King carried a dying girl to her mother. The Yankee then saw
him as heroic.
    As they were peregrinating, the Yankee decided that the king's
palliation was that he was harmless, however proud he was. For example, as they were being sold, the Yankee had to assuage Arthur,
who was demurring that he was the King. The Yankee's action
was neither pusillanimous or ignominous, but necessary to prevent
them from getting into trouble.
    The cul-de-sac, Arthur, has a porlous start because of the fact
that he is the King. However, on the road with the Yankee, he
is no more than a peasant, and learns the hard life of the poor.
    At the gallows in London, the King was about to be hung. The
Yankee realized then how he felt about the king, and dropped his
aspereties concerning the king, who had obviously changed as a
result of the journey, and replaced them with laudations for the
king's goodness, which previously had been overshadowed by his
nobility. Just as the king was about to be killed, the Yankee ran
to try to rescue him. It was unnecessary; Sir Launcelot and the
"boys" wearing helmets with copse-like plumes, rode in on bi-
cycles, to the rescue. (ninth grade English).

There is a pointlessness in much such writing, a feeling that the student is
simply repeating what is already known with little involvement or sense of
purpose. Often, it is sufficient to list the facts, as in the first two examples, or
to provide strings of loosely related illustrations, as in the third. The fourth
example is a test of a different sort, requiring a display of newly (and still
uncomfortably) acquired vocabulary in the process of summarizing a recent
reading assignment.
    Overall, 48 percent of the writing samples provided by the teachers were
categorized as informational writing to the teacher as examiner. More specifically, the most frequent task involved analysis directed to the teacher as

examiner; this accounted for 22 percent of all of the writing collected. (See table 29, Appendix 1.)

Papers addressed to a "wider audience" usually involve more naturally motivated tasks, where there are new items of information or new experiences to convey to someone who does not already know about them. We defined this category very generally, to include everything from publishable, sophisticated writing to notes and letters to specific friends. Even with this broad definition, only 12 percent of school writing was categorized as being addressed to a wider audience. Writing from business education was most likely to fall into this category, reflecting the various form letters (and letter formats) that business students learn. Letters were sometimes used in other subjects areas as well:

Olympia, WA 98503
April 30, 1980
President Jimmy Carter
The White House
1600 Pennsylvania Avenue
Washington, D.C. 20500

Mr. President,

In my opinion, boycotting the Olympic games in Moscow will not solve the United States' problems. It may be a good decision on your part (if our allies join us) because it would and will cost the Russians a good deal of money. But in the case that our European allies do not join us, it will have no effect on the U.S.S.R. I also feel that you're not considering the feelings of our athletes. Yes, you may have apologized to them, but apologies will not take away the four hard years of preparations for these 1980 Summer Olympic Games.

As you know, to compete in the Olympics, an athlete must be an amateur there, spending their own money and time. Your decision to boycott the Olympics might be more applicable if the United States paid the athletes what they have spent and for the time they have used to train for the Olympics. I agree that the athletes wanted no money when they were training and planning to go to the Olympics, but a Gold Medal in the athlete's event, representing your country, is something that money can't buy.

I think the United States should compete in the 1980 Summer Olympics, because we are very lucky to have very talented athletes. If we did go, I am sure the United States' athletes would return with many medals showing the United States' superiority there. When a gold medal was won by one of our athletes, they would not have to attend the ceremonies.

However, Mr. President, I am glad that I am not in your position, because I might not feel this way now.

Thank you for listening to my opinion.

Sincerely,

(ninth grade Social Science)

Stories, when they were approached with some involvement on the part of the writer, were another type of writing which moved out of the school context to address a wider audience:

> The snow was falling up in the mountains where the hawks were flying above in the distance. Down below the wind was whistling through the cracks in the log walls of the cabin. The river was frozen from snowbank to snowbank. On the other side of the river a large buck was chewing on the bark of a tree. Off in the distance I heard a noise, a loud gunshot. The buck suddenly ran off swiftly but quietly in the snow. There was no sound at all as I watched the snow being kicked up behind the buck. The next thing I heard was a scratchy loud voice that said, "Damn . . . How could I a missed that?" I looked in the direction of the voice, and down from a hill, through the flakes of falling snow, was a man, an old man with a long white beard. He stopped and slowly poured some gunpowder down the barrel of the gun, it looked as if he was keeping one eye on me as the other watched his hand while he put a lead ball in the barrel, he packed it good and tight with a long rod, he took the rod out of the barrel and put it in a slot on the gun just beneath the barrel. My head grew light and my feet got cold as the man raised the gun. I felt sweat running down my face when I heard the click of the hammer lock in the back position. Now it was as if I was the buck with a fifty caliber flintlock aimed at me. My legs were too stiff to run and my mind was too far off to tell them to. The old man screamed in laughter as he withdrew his rifle and yelled, "What's the matter, ya frade of an old fool like me, are ya?" I didn't or I couldnt say a word to the old man. (eleventh grade English)

Finally, some 17 percent of the writing from science classes was addressed to a wider audience, reflecting reports in which students described their own experiments and became excited about and involved with their findings. The excerpts below, from the conclusion of a paper that explored oceanic farming as an answer to the world's food problems, reflect such an enthusiasm:

> As a result of having done research at the Dauphin Island Sea Lab this summer, and from further investigations through library resources, I have concluded that one of the most important steps in developing marine farming, would be to follow the principles of ecology by working and co-operating with nature in an effort to establish balanced, stable communities rather than supporting large crops artificially, as we do on land whose side effects are already devastatingly disastrous.
>
> Man's most exciting challenge in marine farming, at the moment, would be to grasp the opportunity of making a new start in the development of food production and putting to use the ecological knowledge that we already have.
>
> Modern advances in technology usually generate wide-spread threats to the environment, but it is very enlightening to know that using water from the sea for either food production, power

or even to obtain fresh water is a pollution free process. Vast areas of our planet could be put to use in the field of marine farming if only we will stop and attempt to take advantage of our inexhaustible supply of knowledge that we already have about the ocean. That great body of water which is man's answer to the already existing food shotage. (eleventh grade Biology)

Though writing addressed to wider audiences was relatively rare in the samples provided by the teachers in this study, it was evidently valued by them. Some 17 percent of the papers rated by the teachers as among the top quarter were categorized as addressed to a wider audience, compared with only 6 percent of the papers from among the bottom quarter of those received. (The difference was significant at the .05 level, chi-square for correlated proportions = 4.0, df = 1.)

Length of Writing Assignments

Teachers were asked several questions about the length of writing assignments they made. Their responses are summarized in table 14. The most typical writing assignment reported by these teachers was a page or less, though some 47 percent of the English teachers and 20 percent or more of the science and social science teachers reported "typically" assigning up to two pages. Longer assignments were made occasionally in all subjects, but particularly in English and the social sciences. Though differences between grade levels were slight, assignments of over two pages were significantly more likely in grade eleven than in grade nine, as were long-term writing assignments (taking a month or more).

When teachers were asked how much time students were given to complete a typical assignment, 52 percent indicated the typical assignment was due within two days; 91 percent reported that the typical assignment was due within a week or less. Subject-area and grade-level differences were slight, except that writing in math classes was more likely to be due the day it was assigned.

Student reports of the amount of time actually spent on writing were similar: 50 percent of the writing they discussed had been completed in an hour or less; only 13 percent had taken a week or more, in spite of a bias in the interview toward discussion of substantial rather than routine work.

Summary

This chapter has taken a first and very general look at the nature of the writing tasks students are being asked to undertake. Results from both the observational studies and the national survey indicate that the use of written language

Table 14

Length of Writing Assignments

| | Percent of Teachers Reporting[1] | | | | | | | | Chi-square tests[2] | |
| | Subject Area | | | | | | Grade | | | |
Length	English n=139	Foreign Language n=69	Math n=18	Science n=87	Social Science n=101	Business n=54	Ninth n=221	Eleventh n=235	Subject df=10	Grade df=2
Up to 250 words (one page)										
Occasionally	28.1	24.6	38.9	51.7	39.6	42.6	31.7	41.7	59.55***	5.29
Typically	59.7	60.9	0.0	32.2	41.6	50.0	52.5	43.0		
251 to 500 words (one to two pages)										
Occasionally	40.3	30.4	11.1	36.8	44.6	33.3	36.2	38.7	107.41***	0.32
Typically	46.8	4.3	5.6	19.5	24.8	9.3	25.3	24.7		
501 to 1000 words (two to four pages)										
Occasionally	45.3	8.7	11.1	29.9	41.6	14.8	29.0	35.3	71.16***	8.80*
Typically	10.8	2.9	5.6	4.6	13.9	0.0	5.0	10.6		
Over 1000 words (more than four pages)										
Occasionally	35.3	7.2	11.1	17.2	31.7	5.6	17.2	28.9	51.18***	12.92**
Typically	3.6	0.0	0.0	3.4	6.9	0.0	1.8	4.7		

| | Percent of Teachers Reporting[1] | | | | | | | | Chi-square tests[2] | |
| | Subject Area | | | | | | Grade | | | |
Length	English n=139	Foreign Language n=69	Math n=18	Science n=87	Social Science n=101	Business n=54	Ninth n=221	Eleventh n=235	Subject df=10	Grade df=2
Long term writing assignments (taking a month or more)[2]	46.0	20.0	17.6	30.7	54.5	12.5	31.1	41.4	45.73***	5.22*

1. Includes only teachers who assign writing of at least paragraph length.
2. Chi-square tests are based on three-point scales: never assigned, occasionally assigned, assigned typically.
3. n=139, 70, 17, 88, 101, 56, 222, 237; df=5, 1
* p < .05; ** p < .01; *** p < .001

to record information for later reference is an important part of the curriculum in virtually all subject areas, taking up some 44 percent of observed class time.

The nature of much of this activity is sharply restricted, however; only some 3 percent of observed class time involved writing of at least paragraph length; even in English classes, the traditional center for writing instruction, only about 10 percent of class time was devoted to writing in this sense. Results from the national survey suggested similar emphases. Writing-related activities reported in frequent use were weighted toward mechanical writing tasks; only about a third of the teachers reported frequently asking students to write at greater length.

When students were asked to write a paragraph or more, the task usually involved informational writing of a page or less in length, to be graded by the teacher. The needs of the different subject areas led to differences in their emphasis on the various kinds of informational writing, and overall there was a slight but statistically significant movement toward longer and more abstract writing between ninth and eleventh grade.

The following chapters will place these assignments into the instructional contexts from which they derive, trace the goals which teachers claim for writing in their classes, and examine the way those goals interact with the assignments given and the teaching techniques adopted.

4 Purposes for Assigning Writing

In understanding the kinds of writing that students are assigned, it is helpful to relate the writing tasks to the instructional context out of which the tasks emerge. In this and the following chapters, we will explore two different ways of making sense of those contexts: one based on the reasons for asking students to write at all, the other on the kinds of instructional support that teachers feel it necessary to provide for various types of writing tasks.

Developing a Measure of Teachers' Purposes

Studying 246 British teachers from various subject areas, Barnes and Shemilt (1974) found that a large number of separate attitudes and teaching practices could be interpreted in terms of two sharply polarized views of the writing process. Some teachers saw writing primarily as a way to encode and repeat a traditional body of knowledge; Barnes and Shemilt called this the *transmission* view of the writing process. Other teachers took an *interpretation* view of writing, seeing it as a way for the student to explore a subject area and gain understanding of new concepts in the process of writing about them. These views shaped diverse aspects of instruction, including the types of writing requested, the help provided while students were writing, marking and assessment of the completed writing, and the nature and extent of follow up work.

Barnes and Shemilt's results seemed promising, but their use of content analysis of open-ended responses was not appropriate for the present study. Hence one of our tasks was to design a scale that would measure the extent to which teachers adhered to a "transmission" or "interpretation" view of writing. For the pilot study, twelve contrasting purposes for writing were drawn from Barnes and Shemilt's report, and teachers were asked to rate each purpose on a four-point scale from "not important" to "very important" for the particular class.

As we might have expected with this format, responses were dominated by the general importance which teachers placed on writing activities; any other differences in their attitudes were minimized. A variety of exploratory factor analyses was undertaken to examine residual patterns of variation after the general response pattern was taken into account. Two secondary dimensions emerged from these analyses. One was defined by such goals as "to help students remember important information" and "to discover whether students have learned relevant content"; at the opposite pole of the same dimension was "to correlate personal experience with the topic being considered." The second dimension was defined by such items as "to explore material not covered in class" and "to force students to think for themselves," contrasted with "writing to provide writing practice." Though the pilot version of these questions was unsatisfactory, the scales made intuitive sense as, roughly, (1) a stress on subject-area information versus personal experience, and (2) a stress on the application of subject-area concepts versus the development of writing skills.

Accordingly, the question format was changed from a four-point scale to a series in which teachers were asked to indicate the most important and least important reasons for assigning writing in a particular class. (During computer analysis, these responses were converted into a three-point scale for each item.) Items were rewritten to remove ambiguities, clarify the factor structure, and more equally represent the hypothesized underlying dimensions. The final version of the questionnaire had twelve items related to reasons for assigning writing, three for each pole of the two hypothesized dimensions.

After teachers in the national sample had completed the questionnaire, their responses to this series of items were similarly factor analyzed. Table 15 summarizes the results. The first factor contrasts writing tasks which focus on subject area information with those that focus on personal or imaginative experience; the second contrasts a stress on developing and applying subject-area concepts with a stress on the mechanics of writing and on clear expression. These results confirm and extend the patterns that emerged from the pilot work.

To provide single measures of these two factors, the six items most strongly related to each factor were summed, with appropriate signs and unit weights. The resulting measures of *stress on information* and *stress on concepts* correlated .27 within the national sample. Alpha coefficients, which provide a measure of internal consistency and reliability, were .67 for information and .58 for concepts.

The Range of Purposes Reported

To get a sense of teachers' usual reasons for asking students to write, the scales were divided into thirds representing high, moderate, and low scores on each continuum. Dividing responses in this way, 70 percent of the teachers emphasized subject-area information in their writing assignments, contrasted with only 16 percent who were primarily concerned with personal experience. Responses on the other dimension were similarly skewed, with 44 percent reflecting concern with concepts and 24 percent concern with writing skills.

Taken together, the scales measuring stress on applying concepts and stress on learning subject-area information define a range of purposes for assigning writing in school. Figure 2 displays these attitudes and plots average scores for each of the six subject areas. These results are elaborated in table 16, which includes a summary of responses to individual items.

English teachers were most likely to stress personal and imaginative experience in their writing assignments, though testing of subject-area content was reported to be an important use of writing in 46 percent of their classrooms. One of the English teachers from the city high school acknowledged this duality in goals:

> I think there are two reasons [for asking students to write], that are not generally connected to each other. One is, I need to know if they are learning what I am teaching for all of the reasons that you know—to grade them, to grade me, to know whether to continue a unit, to judge . . . all of that stuff. And the other one, and

Table 15

Rotated Factor Loadings, Reasons for Asking Students to Write

	Factors[1]	
Reason	Stress on Information	Stress on Concepts
To remember information	.65	.28
To correlate experience with topic	−.62	.17
To test learning of content	.49	−.00
To share imaginative experiences	−.63	−.22
To summarize class material	.64	.04
To express feelings	−.60	−.29
To explore out-of-class material	.10	.46
To practice writing mechanics	−.10	−.70
To force thinking	.03	.53
To apply concepts to new situations	.04	.67
To teach proper essay form	−.00	−.50
To test clear expression	−.12	−.41
Percent of total variation	18.8	17.4

1. Principal components analysis, with rotation of the two largest vectors to the Varimax criterion.

n=734 teachers

the one that I think is more important but probably really isn't, I think it's almost impossible for you to organize what you know and to really understand what you know if you haven't tried to put it down on paper. So let me say it another way; the second reason . . . in order to really understand something, you have to have tried to tell it to someone else, and that's really why I have them write.

English teachers are also, as one might expect, more concerned than teachers of the other subject areas with clear expression, writing mechanics, and proper essay form. Foreign language teachers show a similar concern with the mechanics of writing (though presumably in the foreign language), but place more emphasis on subject-area material and less on personal experience than do the English teachers.

Math and science teachers' attitudes fall at the other extreme. In their writing assignments, they are primarily concerned with a combination of subject-area information and the application of concepts to new situations. It is in the application of concepts that essay writing really becomes valuable, offering an opportunity that short-answer and other mechanical formats do not provide.

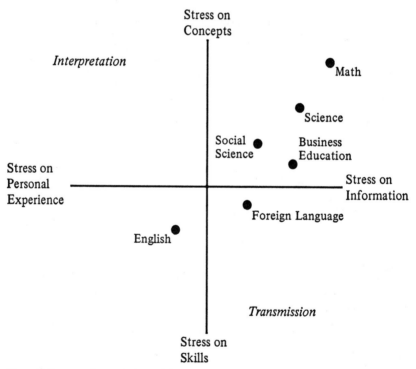

Figure 2. Purposes for assigning writing.

As one science teacher explained:

> Yes, it's important for them to know the content of the area, yet I feel they need practice writing in each subject area. Also in some essay questions they can draw many areas of knowledge together to form their answers.

Business education and social science teachers, as groups, fell somewhat in the middle of the scale, both placing some emphasis on subject-area knowledge; and both were relatively balanced in their stress on writing skills versus the application of concepts. The mix of goals was evident in a business education teacher's comments on what she looks for in grading papers:

> If we are talking about the business letters in Communication, I see if the purpose of the letter has been attended to. If someone could follow what needs to be done without contacting the person or without other communication. In terms of the term paper, in content I looked at the areas which we proposed that the students should touch on and I . . . to see if those were well-covered . . . I looked at the course outline to see if they actually dealt with what they set out to deal with. . . . I always look at [writing mechanics]. All kinds of errors are marked—grammatical errors, punctuation, spelling—I always mark those.

The Writing Students Do, Revisited

Teachers' goals in assigning writing tasks are directly related to the kinds of assignments they give. Overall, writing of at least paragraph length was more likely to be assigned by teachers who stressed personal experience (63 percent reporting frequent use) rather than subject-area information (18 percent), and also by those who emphasized writing skills (48 percent) rather than the application of concepts (16 percent) (see table 30, Appendix 1). These reports were confirmed by another series of questions, which asked what percentage of the mark on the final examination would be based on responses requiring paragraph length writing. (Whatever teachers may say they stress, the tasks they set on examinations are a very direct statement of the skills they value.) Table 17 summarizes results for those teachers who planned to give a final exam at all.

For the sample as a whole, an average of 16 percent of the grade on the final examination was based on questions that required writing of at least paragraph length. Teachers who stressed both personal experience and writing skills gave the most prominence to such questions, using them as the basis of 40 percent of the examination grade; those who stressed both subject-area information and the application of concepts gave least prominence to questions requiring paragraph-length writing, using them for an average of only 7 percent of the exam grade.

Table 16

Reasons for Asking Students to Write

Reasons	Percent of Teachers Rating as One of Two "Most Important"								Chi-square tests[1]	
	Subject Area						Grade			
	English n=140	Foreign Language n=102	Math n=142	Science n=134	Social Science n=113	Business n=102	Ninth n=377	Eleventh n=345	Subject df=10	Grade df=2
Stress on information versus personal experience										
To remember information	18.6	53.9	91.5	67.2	56.6	72.5	62.1	56.5	208.1***	2.71
To correlate experience with topic	47.1	24.5	3.5	11.9	16.8	8.8	20.7	18.3	119.20***	2.35
To test learning of content	45.7	57.8	58.5	71.6	61.9	63.9	57.8	61.4	48.77***	6.17*
To share imaginative experiences	30.0	12.7	0.0	1.5	3.5	2.0	8.2	8.4	189.18***	0.11
To summarize class material	13.6	31.4	47.9	39.6	38.9	33.3	33.2	34.5	165.23***	0.27
To express feelings	38.6	22.5	2.1	10.4	27.4	15.7	21.2	17.4	124.78***	3.73
Stress on concepts versus skills										
To explore out-of-class material	5.0[2]	8.8	13.1[3]	23.9	28.3	10.8	18.7[4]	10.9[5]	131.83***	8.85*
To practice writing mechanics	46.8[2]	65.7	5.1[3]	6.7	15.9	35.3	29.0[4]	26.4[5]	205.18***	1.42
To force thinking	44.0[2]	30.4	75.2[3]	58.2	62.8	50.0	52.3[4]	57.2[5]	60.75***	1.73
To apply concepts to new situations	22.0[2]	48.0	70.8[3]	59.7	38.1	48.0	46.3[4]	49.7[5]	94.59***	1.16
To teach proper essay form	27.7[2]	5.9	2.9[3]	14.2	18.6	23.5	14.9[4]	15.8[5]	77.53***	4.07
To test clear expression	61.0[2]	46.1	29.2[3]	41.8	38.9	28.4	39.8[4]	42.5[5]	47.68***	0.64

Reasons	Percent of Teachers Rating as One of Two "Most Important"								Chi-square tests[1]		F-Statistics		
	Subject Area						Grade		Subject df=10	Grade df=2	Subject df=5;685	Grade df=1;685	Inter-action df=5;685
	English n=140	Foreign Language n=102	Math n=142	Science n=134	Social Science n=113	Business n=102	Ninth n=377	Eleventh n=345					
Summed Scores					Averages								
Stress on information	-1.0	1.6	3.8	3.1	2.1	2.8	2.0	2.1			84.65***	0.14	0.63
Stress on concepts	-1.3	-0.5	2.5	1.6	1.0	0.5	0.7	0.6			53.01***	0.41	2.03

Multivariate Analysis of Variance (for 12 scales)

Effect	Lambda	df	F-Statistic
Subject	0.34	60;3183	13.82***
Grade	0.96	12;679	2.18*
Interaction	0.91	60;3183	1.03

1. Chi-square tests are based on three-point scales.
2. n=141
3. n=137
4. n=369
5. n=348

* $p < .05$; ** $p < .01$; *** $p < .001$

66   *Writing in the Secondary School*

Tables 18 and 19 summarize relationships between teachers' general purposes in making writing assignments, the types of writing assigned, and the audience to whom the writing was to be directed.

Whatever their specific views of the purposes of asking students to write, teachers in all groups emphasized informational writing: reporting on particular events, summarizing a series of particular events, analyzing, and theorizing. Within this general pattern, teachers who were concerned with the application of subject-area concepts were more likely to assign writing tasks involving theorizing, while teachers whose primary concern was with subject-area information were more likely to assign long-term writing projects. A consumer education teacher who used a variety of information-oriented mechanical writing tasks made explicit why she also valued project work:

> *What writing do your students do?*
> I would say that some take notes and I give written work for them to do such as check sheets, worksheets, a lot of times it is only true/false that they write or something like that. Other times they have to write definitions for like fill-in-the-blanks, crossword puzzles . . . that type of writing. All of my tests are multiple choice, true/false, and matching type. I have not given any exams that are essay, but I do give extra credit questions which are essay type. Then I have students do things like summarize an article, which

Table 17

Average Percent of Final Exam Reported Based on Writing

	Stress on Information		
Stress on Concepts	Low n=90	Moderate n=83	High n=430
Low (n=132)	40.0	30.3	16.5
Moderate (n=193)	36.2	21.3	13.0
High (n=278)	22.3	20.8	7.0

Analysis of Variance	
Effect	F-Statistic
Information (df=2; 594)	39.740***
Concepts (df=2; 594)	12.018***
Interaction (df=4; 594)	0.872

* $p < .05$; ** $p < .01$; *** $p < .001$

Table 18

Relationships between Teachers' Purposes and Types of Writing Assigned

Type of Writing	Percent of Teachers Reporting[1]						Chi-square test	
	Stress on Information			Stress on Concepts				
	High n=261	Moderate n=84	Low n=107	High n=141	Moderate n=171	Low n=140	Information df=2	Concepts df=2
Informational								
Report	67.8	83.3	76.6	75.2	70.8	72.9	8.77*	0.76
Summary	70.5	59.5	66.4	73.0	66.7	63.6	3.57	3.02
Analysis	75.1	82.1	76.6	80.9	75.4	73.6	1.77	2.26
Theory	62.1	60.7	53.3	67.4	62.6	48.6	2.48	11.25**
Personal	32.2	51.2	72.0	29.8	45.6	60.0	50.02***	25.92****
Imaginative	26.8	57.1	77.6	29.1	46.2	57.9	85.86****	23.89****
Other	21.5	16.7	22.4	17.0	19.9	27.1	1.11	4.60
Long term writing assignments (taking a month or more)[2]	43.4	44.3	30.7	33.3	36.0	39.9	8.54*	1.36

1. Includes only teachers who assign writing of at least paragraph length.
2. n=277, 88, 106, 150, 178, 143
*p < .05; **p < .01; ***p < .001

Table 19

Relationships between Teachers' Purposes and Audiences for Writing

| Audience | Percent of Teachers Reporting[1] | | | | | | Chi-square test | |
| | Stress on Information | | | Stress on Concepts | | | Information df=2 | Concepts df=2 |
	High n=279	Moderate n=87	Low n=107	High n=151	Moderate n=178	Low n=144		
Only the student	47.0	35.6	48.6	47.7	44.9	43.1	4.06	0.65
Teacher, to react without assigning a grade	64.9	73.6	74.8	64.2	73.0	67.4	4.69	3.05
Teacher, to grade without other comment	55.9	48.3	34.6	61.6	50.0	38.9	14.17***	15.21***
Teacher, to react and grade	95.0[2]	97.7	95.3	96.7	96.1[3]	94.4	1.16	0.99
Other students	44.4	60.9	79.4	47.7	55.6	64.6	39.65***	8.54*
Others	8.6	8.0	14.0	6.6	8.4	15.3	2.93	6.90*

1. Includes only teachers who assign writing of at least paragraph length.

2. n=280

3. n=179

* p < .05; ** p < .01; *** p < .001

is a one-page summary. The better students do projects, and this is on the basis of pretest, and if they do a project, a lot of time it would be more like a research paper.

Why do you assign this type of writing?
One of my goals is to save time, and so that saves me some.

The largest differences in types of writing assigned, however, were in the areas of personal and imaginative writing. Both of these were at least twice as likely to be assigned by teachers who stressed individual experience rather than subject-area information, and by teachers who stressed writing skills rather than the application of concepts. These same teachers were also more likely to provide wider audiences for writing, particularly to offer opportunities for students to read one another's work. Conversely, they were less likely to simply assign a grade to a writing assignment, without other comment.

A science teacher provided us with a useful reminder that "good" writing can take many different forms:

> There is a certain way in which [science] papers have to be written in order to be published and I've tried to follow with some of them this particular format and try to show them how this writing is different from others. Which brings out a point which was a problem to me a few years back. I had a student who went to the state competition, and won outstanding in the state. The scientific paper was well-written, he had aspiration of being in science—this is his area—and he said he wanted to go into it. He was doing excellent . . . he could use subordinate clauses . . . I thought there was nothing wrong with the way he was writing, his grammar, and everything else as far as English was concerned. Yet he was failing his English class in ninth grade because he was not creative. The young man did not want to be creative, he wanted to be scientific. So I think students need to know that there is more than one type of writing . . . and some learn to write poems while others would just as soon write a scientific paper and do quite well with it. And we never could convince this young man to be creative, and I believe he ended up failing freshman English.

Of the many implications that might be drawn from these comments, the mixture of definitions of "good writing" seems especially important to note. On the one hand there is a tendency to equate good writing with sentence-level skills ("he could use subordinate clauses," "there was nothing wrong with the way he was writing, his grammar"). On the other, there is a recognition that the writing of science has its own particular conventions and ways of proceeding which are quite different from those that matter in English class (here equated with creative writing, particularly poetry). Such a mix of views, of understandings and misunderstandings, would provide an excellent starting point for any discussion of the place of writing instruction within the curriculum as a whole.

Who Should Teach Writing

The reasons teachers cited for asking students to write were closely related to the extent to which they saw themselves as responsible for the teaching of writing in their subject area. Overall, some 82 percent of the teachers felt that both the subject-area teacher and the English teacher should take responsibility for the development of writing skills; only 18 percent felt that this should be the sole responsibility of the English teacher. Attitudes were somewhat be-grudging, however; some teachers failed to realize that writing in their subjects might contribute to subject-area learning as well as to the English teacher's task. Such an attitude seems to underlie the following comment, also from a science teacher:

> We in the sciences and social sciences should allow them to prac-
> tice their writing skills, try what we can to improve their skills, but
> I do think most of it falls on the English teacher as far as working
> with the grammar and trying to show them how to express them-
> selves on paper.

In the national survey, mathematics teachers were least willing to share the responsibility of teaching students to write, 32 percent claiming this should be the English teachers' job. English teachers were the most eager to involve teachers of other subject areas in the problem, only 4 percent claiming the task solely for themselves.

Table 20 relates this concern to teachers' reasons for asking students to write in their classes. Only 8 percent of those who were concerned with the teaching of writing skills limited this concern to English classes, compared with 26 percent of those who used writing primarily to get students to apply concepts in new areas. Similarly only 5 percent of the teachers concerned with students' personal experience felt that the teaching of writing is only the English teacher's responsibility, compared with 21 percent of teachers whose primary concern was with subject-area information. This attitude is particularly clear in the comments of the following teacher, who limited her concern to the conventions of specialized forms of writing in her subject area:

> *Who do you think is responsible for teaching students to write?*
> Basically, I think it starts in the elementary, and like I said, most
> students who write now, by the time they are in high school, they
> are either highly motivated to do that and want to improve, or
> they are just in the habit of already writing well. So, I don't feel
> any real strong responsibility.
>   Now, in my foods classes I do feel a certain responsibility. That
> they spell for instance words that are used in foods only, they
> might be used other places but they are definitely foods words
> kinds of things.

Also certain mechanics like writing a menu, center it to capital-
ized words, to put it in one particular order, a nice looking paper.
So in measuring writing recipes, writing work plans, I do teach
them writing in that class.

In Consumer Ed I feel that the students in the class are there
basically to learn the attitude and the ideas rather than to write it.

I do think it makes a difference in what class you're teaching
as to whether or not you stress things like spelling, punctuation,
correction.

Like the science teacher whose prize student had failed English, this teacher
recognizes some specialized conventions of writing that are specific to her
subject area, and considers it her responsibility to teach these conventions.
Yet the two teachers are a long way apart in their conceptualization of those
specialized writing skills. For the science teacher, the skills seem part of a
whole approach to the subject; the student he was discussing "did not want
to be creative, he wanted to be scientific." This is quite a different conception of content-area writing skills than that of teaching students to spell the
specialized vocabulary of food classes or to master the mechanics of writing
a menu.

Table 20

Relationships between Teachers' Purposes
and Perceived Responsibility for Teaching Writing

Purposes	N	Percent of Teachers Indicating		
		English Teacher	Subject Area Teacher	Both Are Responsible
Stress on Information				
High	515	21.4	0.4	78.3
Moderate	102	13.7	1.0	85.3
Low	119	5.0	0.8	94.1
Stress on Concepts				
High	316	25.6	0.3	74.1
Moderate	234	12.8	0.9	86.3
Low	179	8.4	0.6	91.1

Chi-square test (df=4): Information=19.54***; Concepts=29.11***
* $p < .05$; ** $p < .01$; *** $p < .001$

Summary

A series of scales was developed to measure the major dimensions underlying teachers' purposes in assigning writing tasks. Although the instrument was based upon Barnes and Shemilt's (1974) study of the attitudes of British teachers, the results were more complex than the earlier work would have suggested. Rather than a simple polarization of attitudes, two dimensions were found. The first appears to contrast the learning of subject-area information with the exploration of the personal or imaginative experience of the student. The second contrasts assignments designed to develop students' writing skills with those demanding the application of concepts in new situations.

These dimensions were in turn related in systematic (and intuitively sensible) ways to the characteristics of the assigned writing, including the relationship between the writing task and the experiences being written about (that is, the function of the writing, in Britton's [1970] sense), and the audience to whom the writing was addressed.

We should note, however, that the two dimensions underlying teachers' responses represent the way that writing is currently viewed, rather than a necessary set of choices among instructional goals. It is quite possible to argue that in effective instructional contexts the polarities might collapse: that the most effective learning of writing skills occurs when concepts are being applied, or that subject-area information is learned best when applied in the context of individual experience. These are issues that we will return to later.

5 Writing Instruction

This chapter describes processes and procedures that teachers employ when they assign writing of any substantial length. The focus is on teaching: how the differing procedures teachers adopt help their students learn. The problem in such a description is to avoid triviality. There are innumerable procedures that may be used in conjunction with writing assignments, a variety which may be necessary to maintain interest and effectiveness. But any attempt to explore broad characteristics of instruction and their relationship to the writing that results becomes bewildering in its detail. The approach taken in the present study has already been introduced in chapter 1. We have viewed particular teaching techniques in light of their relationship to the composing process, particularly in light of the kind of instructional support which the techniques provide for that process.

In this context, mechanical writing tasks (such as multiple-choice and fill-in-the-blank exercises) can be seen as tasks in which the support is so complete that the problem of composing coherent text has been taken over by the teacher, leaving the student to supply only the appropriate items of information. Similarly, writing in a test situation, where the only prompts are likely to be an essay title and some indication of appropriate length, can be seen as an instance where no instructional support is provided at all, leaving the students to work through the entire process on their own. It is only slightly paradoxical to suggest that these two extremes—the one providing no support for the writing task and the other taking over almost all of it—are likely to be characteristic of the writing assignments in the same group of classrooms.

Prewriting

One of the most critical places in a writing task, from both the teacher's and the pupil's point of view, is the beginning, which includes making the topic clear and conveying expectations about the dimensions of the task: such details as length and form as well as the boundaries of students' relevant knowledge and experience.

Setting the Topic

The importance of the expectations conveyed at this stage is evident in one ninth grader's reaction to a report-writing assignment in science:

> Well, I was disappointed because he didn't give us—I didn't feel
> that he gave me enough information on what he wanted me to
> write about. It was like he turned me loose on something that
> looked rather important to him, 'cause it's only like the second one
> we've had all year and it didn't give me enough information. . . .
> he said we needed two other references besides our biology book,
> it was worth 100 points, and he had given us five days to do it in,
> or four days to do it, so it seemed to me like he meant it to be an
> important assignment. But with what he wrote down—the infor-
> mation it was—I could of easily done it in a page. He said three pages
> and I really was baffled. (Bart, grade nine, laboratory school)

Bart's reaction to being "turned loose" on an unfamiliar topic is under-
standable, though his comments about the way in which the assignment was
presented to him make it sound typical of the way in which secondary school
students are asked to write. In the observational studies, the amount of time
devoted to prewriting activities averaged just over three minutes. That included
everything from the time the teacher began introducing the topic until the
first student began to write. Those three minutes were spent writing the essay
topic on the board, or passing out and reading through a dittoed assignment
sheet, followed by student questions about task dimensions: "How long does
it have to be?" "Can I write in pencil?" "Do I *have* to do this?"

Though the way Bart was asked to write his science report was typical of
many other assignments, the task itself was unusual in several respects. In the
previous chapter, we noted the extent to which teachers in all subject areas
emphasized writing as a way to test students' knowledge of subject-area information and concepts; in such situations, the task for the student is one of
organizing and reporting back information that is already available. Delineating
the topic is straight-forward and students know what they are supposed to do.

Listed below is a variety of writing assignments which function in this way,
drawn from responses to the national survey and from the observational study.
Characteristically, the topics are in one sense impossible, deserving book-length
treatment to be handled well. They become reasonable tasks only when they
are interpreted by the student as requests to summarize material previously
presented in lessons or texts.

> Western Europe on the eve of the Reformation was a civilization
> going through great changes. In a well-written essay describe the
> political, economic, social, and cultural changes Europe was going
> through at the time of the Reformation. (25 points)
>   (ninth grade Social Studies)
> Select some phase of twentieth-century American literature and
> discuss it in a theme of 300–500 words. Turn in polished draft only.
>   (eleventh grade English)
> Write a one-page report on one of the following topics. Please be
> neat with your work. Check for spelling and sentence structure.

1. the diesel engine
2. the gas engine
3. supersonic flight
4. sound
5. what can I do to conserve fuel?

(ninth grade Science)

Explain the ability of the Constitution to change with the times.

(eleventh grade American History)

Write a paragraph on solving quadratic equations.

(ninth grade Algebra)

In a well-organized essay of 200–250 words, answer the question which follows: Homer considered that Odysseus was a hero, a representative of Greek ideals. How is Odysseus a model for youths of all times?

(ninth grade English)

Write a brief essay describing a building (or type of building) which best represents 20th century American culture.

(ninth grade World History)

The marriage vows say, "Until death do us part." According to Toffler, what is the problem? What solutions are likely in the future? Please explain "serial marriage" and "marriage trajectory" as part of your answer. (20 minutes)

(eleventh grade Social Studies)

Define poetry.

(ninth grade English)

Sarah (grade eleven, laboratory school) comments on the limitations of such writing tasks, and contrasts them with writing a long term paper, which is "a time consuming, complicated process that requires a great deal of thought":

> Writing a posttest essay is an easier process because I do not have as many options as when I am writing a term paper. When I write a term paper I can look for what I need and then I must organize. A posttest essay is based on what I already know. Therefore, my options are more limited.
>
> First, what I will write about is limited to a certain subject so that eliminates the problem of picking a subject. I do not research it but instead I must consider what I know my topic is based on my information rather than having to look up information for a topic. Then I must organize my information and hopefully support my theses. This process is quicker because my subject is limited, my knowledge is limited, and my time is also limited. So, there are fewer complications.

The science report that Bart was asked to write, on the other hand, differs in two substantial ways from such "posttest essays." First, although Bart is concerned about the information the teacher "gave" him on the topic, there is a clear suggestion that the students are to find new material on their own. And second, the report format is itself relatively unfamiliar; Bart says that this was only the second such assignment during the year. It is likely to have been these aspects of the task which caused his bewilderment, and which made the teacher's method of giving the assignment, though typical, seem inadequate.

Conveying Task Dimensions

Closely related to the problem of setting the topic for writing assignments is that of defining the dimensions of the task: Who will be the audience for the writing? What is its function or purpose? How will it be evaluated? Certain aspects of the task always seem clearly defined. The length of an assignment is almost always stated in terms of paragraphs or pages or number of points; so too is the time-frame for completing the task. Audience is rarely mentioned, perhaps because the audience for school writing is so universally the teacher, usually in the role of examiner.

On other aspects of the task, teachers sometimes send mixed signals. On the one hand, they tend to complain about the quality of student writing, defining quality largely in terms of sentence-level mechanical skills. On the other hand, particularly in the content areas, they mark the students for subject-area content and provide little guidance about how to approach an assignment. Thus a science teacher, when asked if she does anything to prepare students for the writing assignments she gives, replied:

> Not usually. I expect them to have the skills as far as being able to form paragraphs, know when to use a paragraph, write in complete sentences, this sort of thing, and I tell them ahead of time that they should do this.

Table 21 summarizes student interview responses when they were asked about teacher instructions and their own prewriting activities. (Each student reported on writing in two subject areas; only English and social studies were discussed frequently enough to summarize separately.) Over two-thirds of the students noted instructions related to the form—such things as length, neatness, and layout on the page. All other sorts of instructions were rare in both subject areas. Specific hints as to the appropriate content were reported just over a fourth of the time, teacher-supplied outlines were reported just over 10 percent of the time, and there was occasional discussion of the topic or of model responses. In general, the students' responses are similar to the observers' findings that prewriting activities typically took about three minutes—not time for much at all.

Students' own activities before they begin to write are dominated by the problem of selecting or narrowing a topic. Kathy (eleventh grade, laboratory school) explained how important this stage is, in the context of discussing research papers:

First of all, a topic must be chosen which can fill enough space and which is interesting. I find that if I am not interested in my topic, I get bored quickly of rewriting and rethinking the subject, and my organization, and therefore the quality of the paper, suffers immensely. Having the topic interest you is the most important quality of the topic, but it is also important for there to be information on it somewhat readily available (although the more interesting it is, the easier you will find it to go to lengths to research it) . . .

For their writing in social studies, students were more likely to search out information from reference materials, in the way Kathy is suggesting; in English, they were more likely to spend their time thinking about the subject, trying to sort out relevant opinions and experiences. Less than a fifth of the students, however, indicated that making an outline was part of this sorting out process.

Some teachers, of course, are more concerned with the teaching of writing and work very hard to provide a variety of prewriting activities. Thus when an English teacher at the city high school was asked about how students were prepared for a written assignment, he put the question in context:

Table 21

Prewriting Instructions and Activities Reported by Students

Prewriting Elements	Percent of Students Indicating	
	English n=31	Social Science n=24
Instructions (Class)		
Form	87.1	66.7
Content	25.8	29.2
Mechanics	16.1	8.3
Model (provided by teacher)	9.7	4.2
Outline (provided by teacher)	9.7	12.5
Discussion related to topic	12.9	4.2
Activities (Individual)		
Selecting a topic or focus	51.6	62.5
Thinking about the subject	54.8	29.2
Using text or other books as resource	16.1	54.2
Taking notes	32.3	29.2
Making an outline	19.4	16.7

I've been doing it all semester. The first day of class I gave them a two-page thing on writing. Just about every day when I lecture about anything, I talk at the end or at the beginning of the lecture about how one might go about expressing whatever it is I'm teaching during that day in a written assignment.

So I gave a sermon once last semester, I read one of Jonathan Edwards' sermons, and at the end of it in talking about the content of the sermon I also talked about how you would go about relating this to religious matters, and so on, in writing.

Plus I've tried always when they are going to write about something to give them a specific, logical sequence of experiences. I ask them to read it, ask them factual questions about it, and I ask them to get in groups and discuss the topic that they are going to be writing about, and then I have them write about it individually.

So, I go from individual, to group, back to the individual.

The sequence he is describing is a blend of many techniques designed to clarify both the content to be written about and the form in which the writing is to be cast. His repertoire of techniques includes modelling of successful task performance, comprehension exercises on new material, group discussion in which students have an opportunity to develop their ideas and talk through their experiences, and formal analysis of the qualities of successful writing.

Survey Results

Teachers in the national survey were asked the extent to which they used a number of specific teaching techniques in the course of asking students to write; responses were limited to writing of at least paragraph length, in contexts other than final examinations (after which there is no opportunity for various kinds of follow up activities). The list of techniques was in no way comprehensive, but provided a sampling of approaches at different points in the writing process.

Table 22 summarizes responses to those items related to setting the assignment and beginning the task.

The most popular technique in helping students get started was to have them begin their writing in class, so that they could ask questions about what was expected if they found themselves in difficulties. This approach was most popular with the English teachers, nearly 80 percent of whom reported that they regularly assign writing in this way; it was least likely to be used by the math teachers (11 percent).

Written assignment sheets to explain the task were used regularly by about a third of the teachers; they were particularly popular in the social sciences where students were likely to be asked to prepare reports based on library research. In the other classes, assignments were usually given orally or written on the board.

Model responses for students to examine—a powerful technique in introducing new forms of writing—were reportedly used regularly in 29 percent of

Table 22

Teaching Techniques: Prewriting

| Technique | Percent of Teachers Using Regularly[1] | | | | | | | | Chi-square tests[2] | |
| | Subject Area | | | | | | Grade | | | |
	English n=140	Foreign Language n=70	Math n=18	Science n=88	Social Science n=99	Business n=56	Ninth n=224	Eleventh n=236	Subject df=10	Grade df=2
Assignment sheet	32.9	20.0	27.8	34.1	47.5	33.9	33.0	35.2	36.28***	1.99
Model responses	32.1	47.1	27.8	17.0	19.2	35.7	29.9	28.0	39.69***	2.64
Beginning in class, to answer questions	77.9	60.0	11.1	33.0	37.4	50.0	60.3	45.3	82.48***	10.77**
Brainstorm with class	37.1	14.3	11.1	10.2	14.1	10.7	19.2	20.3	71.66***	0.19

1. Includes only teachers who assign writing of at least paragraph length.
2. Chi-square tests are based on three-point scales: never, sometimes, regularly.
* $p < .05$; ** $p < .01$; *** $p < .001$

the classes. They were cited most frequently by foreign language teachers (47 percent), least frequently by science teachers (17 percent). Even English teachers, who usually spend so much of their time discussing literary selections, apparently use the selections as writing models only about a third of the time. This may be because students are usually asked to read imaginative selections but to write in the informational mode, analyzing and criticizing the selections they have read.

Finally brainstorming, which is one of many techniques that help students draw upon their knowledge and experience, was reported in regular use by some 37 percent of the English teachers, and by no more than 14 percent in any of the other subject areas.

The only significant grade level difference in these responses involved beginning assignments in class. This decreased from 60 to 45 percent between ninth and eleventh grades, reflecting teachers' confidence that the older students can tackle writing assignments on their own.

If we look at teachers' goals in making writing assignments, we find that a stress on individual experience and (to a lesser extent) a stress on teaching writing skills were associated with beginning the writing assignment in class and with the use of brainstorming techniques to help students bring relevant experiences to bear on a writing topic. (These data are summarized in detail in table 31, Appendix 1.)

Writing and Revising

Most writing instruction takes place before students begin to write, or retrospectively after the writing is complete. There are a few techniques, however, that teachers can use to provide instructional support during the writing task itself, either by segmenting the task or by simply being available as a resource when the student needs help. Table 23 summarizes teachers' reports concerning their use of three such techniques.

Though none of the techniques is widely used, having students write in class in order to help them while they are writing is the most frequent. Nearly three quarters of the English teachers and half of the business education and foreign language teachers report regular inclass writing, compared with a quarter or fewer of the science, social science, and mathematics teachers. However, one of the most frequent contexts for inclass writing is the essay exam, during which the technique loses its effectiveness as an instructional procedure and becomes one of monitoring behavior.

Breaking assignments into smaller, more manageable segments to be completed one at a time can be a very effective way to lead students into more complex writing tasks. There are a number of ways such segmentation can be accomplished, depending upon the nature of the writing task and the skills that

Table 23

Teaching Techniques: Writing and Revising

| Technique | Percent of Teachers Using Regularly[1] | | | | | | | | Chi-square tests[2] | |
| | Subject Area | | | | | | Grade | | | |
	English n=140	Foreign Language n=70	Math n=18	Science n=88	Social Science n=99	Business n=56	Ninth n=224	Eleventh n=236	Subject df=10	Grade df=2
Writing in class	73.6	55.7	16.7	25.0	21.2	53.6	50.0	42.8	128.23***	2.95
Break assignment into steps	35.7	30.0	22.2	30.7	27.3	35.7	40.2	25.0	28.92**	12.48**
Require more than one draft	59.3	24.3	11.1	6.8	10.1	32.1	29.9	28.4	151.82***	0.13

1. Includes only teachers who assign writing of at least paragraph length.
2. Chi-square tests are based on three-point scales: never, sometimes, regularly.

* $p < .05$; ** $p < .01$; $p < .001$

the students bring to it. On longer assignments, the most common approach observed was to separate such stages as bibliography cards, outline, rough draft, and final draft, often with separate due dates to allow the teacher to review progress and make suggestions before the student moved on to the next stage. On shorter assignments, teachers sometimes segmented the writing itself, providing an outline either of the structure to be followed (thesis statement, supporting details, conclusion) or of the specific issues to be dealt with in the answer (". . . describe the political, economic, social, and cultural changes Europe was going through at the time of Reformation").

Students in special education classes are particularly in need of help in attacking longer writing assignments. Our observers noted some of the most effective use of segmented tasks in such classrooms. In one ninth grade class, for example, students had been given the following assignment:

> *Book Report*
> Use this format and write the book report on a separate sheet of paper.
>
> I. Title
>
> II. Setting (where the story took place)
>
> III. Main characters (list at least 4 and write a sentence describing each).
>
> IV. Write a paragraph (at least 6 sentences) and describe the opening of the book.
>
> V. Write two paragraphs (at least 6 sentences in each paragraph) and describe the middle of the book. Tell what the main character does and what happens to him.
>
> VI. Write 1 paragraph (at least 6 sentences) and describe what happens at the end of the book. (Tell what happens to the main character.)
>
> VII. Write 1 paragraph (at least 4 sentences). Tell how you liked the book and why. Tell if you would recommend the book to anyone else.

This effectively reduced a four-paragraph theme into a series of one-paragraph tasks, preceded by some warming-up exercises. In terms of producing a well-formed text, the warm-up exercises might better have been separated from the paragraph writing, but the task as a whole was quite successful. The following paper, among the best from the class, illustrates the nature of the writing that can result from such an approach:

> *Book Report*
> I. Hot Rod
>
> II. Setting–California 1950s
>
> III. *Bud Crayne*–a guy who has a lot of noledge about cars.
> *Walt Thomas*–He is a freind of Bud Crayne's.

Ralph Osler–He is also a freind of Bud Crayne's.

Officer Oday–a police officer who comes down hard on Bud.

IV. The book opens with Bud Crayne behind the wheels of his car. He has just rounded a curve at fifty miles an hour, when a green car comes up behind him. The car goes by. He took a pencil from behind his ear, jotted the readings from his equipment. He then speeded to sixty, then 70 and on. Then he passed the green car.

V. In the middle of the book, it tells about Bud's life. It tells about how he became a good driver. It tells about his occupation which is being a mechanic at a gas station. It tells about how Bud quit school and was driving at the age of 13. It tells about the divotion Bud has to his car. At his point it tells how office oday cracks down on Bud. It tells about how Walt Thomas makes a bet to Bud that he can't make it to a town call Trenton in thirty minutes for ten dollars.

It tells about how the school is having a teen age rider. It tell about how Officer Oday trys to get Bud in a drivers ed class to help his driving for the rodeo. The book tells that Officer Oday gets a kid who is just learning to take the class. It tells that Bud makes the Trenton run. It shows how he make the Trenton run. And shows Walt up.

VI. At the end of the book it shows the rodeo. It tells all about the rodeo. It tells how the freinds of Bud get killed in a car accident. It showes how the cars that inter the rodeo get certen things they got to do. Bud didn't win first place. Bud had won friend. It made him feel bad.

VI. I like the book. I thoght it had a lot of suspence. Also it had action at the same time.

Such techniques were used regularly by about a third of the teachers surveyed, and were more prevalent in ninth grade than in eleventh grade classes (table 23).

Requiring more than one draft of a writing assignment was reported less frequently, by just under 30 percent of the teachers surveyed. English teachers were most likely to report "regularly" asking students to rewrite (59 percent); science teachers were least likely to do so (7 percent).

The extent to which all three of these techniques were used was directly related to teachers' goals in setting writing tasks. As we have seen with other aspects of their instruction, teachers who stress subject-area information and those who stress the application of concepts in new areas were less likely than others to help students with the writing task. (Detailed results are summarized in table 31, Appendix 1.)

Even when more than one draft is required, students differ widely in the extent to which a second draft means anything more than editorial tidying up. In the excerpt below, Kathy, a very able eleventh grader, treats her drafts as a way to explore and develop her ideas:

At this point, I have done my research, using my thesis and sketchy outline as a guide and I know my topic pretty well, so I sit down and write my paper, very sketchily, from memorizing only approximations of evidence & dates, etc. The dates and specific evidence can be looked up again later. At this point, if the paper is much too long or short, it is time to get worried & expand or narrow my thesis statement and scribble down another sketchy outline and then rough draft. When my rough, rough draft is the proper size, I go away again, to return once again w/ an open mind.

When I return, I reread everything I have so far, my thesis, my evidence, and then my rough draft, and then I proceed to hack it to pieces (figuratively of course!). Paying attention only to subject & very basic organization (such as order of paragraphs), I scribble all over my rough draft in a diff. colored pen or marker until I like what the paper says. Then I rewrite it, on new paper, filling in specific evidence and being more picky about sentence organization and spelling. When this is done, I reread my paper, which should be almost done, and then, if time permits, I leave again. Upon returning w/ an open mind, I reread the paper, correcting spelling errors and changing a few sentences here and there and when all seems well, I recopy it neatly or type it, depending upon the pickiness of my teacher.

Kathy appears to use her drafts to make significant changes in what she says in her writing. Jeremy, also an able eleventh grader, treats the process very differently. He works from a tight outline, to which he has added "the details" from his research:

The actual writing is not that difficult. You just mainly fill in the outline with the information from your notecards and add some of your own style to tie it all together. If you have planned well and done your research everything just falls into place.

Now you're almost finished. All that is left is adding footnotes and a bibliography if they are necessary. You might want to recopy or even type it for neatness.

Student comments about successive drafts suggest that Jeremy is more typical than Kathy in his process. In writing for English, only 23 percent of the students interviewed claimed to make changes that went beyond spelling, mechanics, usage, or vocabulary choice; in writing for the social sciences, one third claimed to make such larger changes. For the majority of the students, use of successive drafts for more than minor editorial changes requires help from the teacher, and that in turn requires extra time and energy from teachers who are already hard pressed.

Postwriting Responses and Activities

Once students have completed their final draft, the writing activity is over but the process of instruction continues through the responses of teachers and other readers. Student writing is primarily directed to the teacher, as we noted in discussing the nature of assigned writing tasks in chapter 3. The teacher has many options about what to do with this writing, however, ranging from what amounts to sentence-by-sentence editing, to comments on the arguments or point of view expressed in the writing, to arranging to share it with other readers.

Marking the Papers

Table 24 summarizes teachers' answers when asked about the techniques they used in reacting to the writing they receive. Teachers gave two sets of responses to these techniques. In the first, they indicated which techniques were most important and which least important for the particular class being discussed. In the second, they indicated which techniques were used routinely, whether or not they were the most important.

Overall, the rank order of the techniques was similar using the two approaches. The most frequent type of response in routine use was to indicate errors in writing mechanics; this was reported by 71 percent of the teachers. It also ranked first among *important* responses for a particular class (47 percent). Techniques that directly engaged the ideas that the student was expressing—posing counterarguments, responding with the teacher's own views, or suggesting related topics the student might explore—were used routinely by no more than a fifth of the teachers; those techniques were also rated as least important among the possible reactions.

Within this general pattern, however, there were subject-area differences. Teachers of English, business education, and foreign language were most likely to claim "marking mechanical errors" and "commenting on style" to be among the important responses, though the majority of teachers in all subject areas except math reported routinely indicating errors in writing mechanics. Errors of fact and accuracy of conclusions were particularly important to the math and science teachers, and to a lesser extent to the social science teachers.

Grade level differences were less evident than those between subject areas. Eleventh graders were somewhat more likely to be held accountable for the accuracy of their work: comments on mechanical errors, errors of fact, and problems in the logic or organization of the piece were more likely to be used routinely at this grade level; suggestions concerning related topics were less likely to be used. This latter shift may reflect a movement away from a teacher-learner dialogue toward an increasing emphasis on the teacher as examiner.

Teachers' responses to writing assignments were also related to their general purposes in giving the assignments. Teachers who stressed the application of concepts were less likely to stress mechanical errors or style, and more likely to be concerned with errors of fact, the accuracy of the conclusions reached, counterarguments, and related topics. Those concerned with subject-area

Table 24

Teacher Responses to Student Writing

| Type of Response | Percent of Teachers Indicating[1] | | | | | | | | Chi-square tests | |
| | Subject Area | | | | | | Grade | | | |
	English n=138	Foreign Language n=70	Math n=18	Science n=88	Social Science n=100	Business n=55	Ninth n=223	Eleventh n=234	Subject df=10	Grade df=2
Important to[2]										
Indicate mechanical errors	56.5	80.0	11.1	25.0	31.0	70.9	46.2	48.7	90.31***	3.44
Suggest improvements in style	62.3	50.0	5.6	5.7	25.0	38.2	38.6	36.3	137.30***	0.49
Point out errors of fact	14.5	31.4	61.1	67.0	62.0	45.5	43.9	41.5	100.34***	5.18
Assess accuracy of conclusion	23.2	14.3	66.7	78.4	51.0	27.3	45.3	36.3	109.69***	5.25
Assign a grade	21.7	42.9	33.3	50.0	52.0	47.3	36.3	42.3	35.71***	1.71
Comment on logic, organization	62.3	31.4	66.7	39.8	44.0	29.1	42.6	50.0	37.96***	2.89
Pose counter arguments	15.2	10.0	27.8	20.5	29.0	12.7	20.2	17.5	29.07**	0.53
Respond with own views	10.1	5.7	11.1	6.8	14.0	7.3	11.7	7.7	8.00	2.28
Suggest related topics	10.1	27.1	11.1	19.3	21.0	18.2	23.3	13.7	17.82	7.87*

Type of Response	Percent of Teachers Indicating[1]								Chi-square tests	
	Subject Area						Grade			
	English n=138	Foreign Language n=70	Math n=18	Science n=88	Social Science n=100	Business n=55	Ninth n=223	Eleventh n=234	Subject df=5	Grade df=1
Routinely[3]										
Indicate mechanical errors	87.7	71.4	33.3	62.5	68.0	58.2	65.0	76.1	38.80***	6.72**
Suggest improvements in style	70.3	44.3	16.7	22.7	33.0	41.8	40.8	47.9	65.30***	2.30
Point out errors of fact	69.6	44.3	27.3	76.1	71.0	47.3	57.8	70.1	37.79***	7.43**
Assess accuracy of conclusion	56.5	20.0	50.0	67.0	61.0	34.5	47.5	55.6	47.64***	2.94
Assign a grade	78.3	62.9	55.6	76.1	67.0	65.5	67.3	73.1	10.54	1.85
Comment on logic, organization	76.1	41.4	61.1	52.3	61.0	30.9	52.0	62.8	44.36***	5.45*
Pose counter arguments	48.6	12.9	16.7	35.2	49.0	18.2	35.4	36.8	43.55***	0.09
Respond with own views	39.9	14.3	5.6	15.9	31.0	23.6	25.6	27.8	28.43***	0.29
Suggest related topics	34.1	24.3	11.1	33.0	41.0	23.6	32.3	32.5	11.35*	0.002

1. Includes only teachers who assign writing of at least paragraph length.
2. Chi-square tests based on three-point scales ranging from most to least important.
3. Chi-square tests based on yes/no responses.

* $p < .05$; ** $p < .01$; *** $p < .001$

information were similarly likely to be concerned about errors of fact and accuracy of conclusions. They were also more likely than other teachers to consider it important to assign a grade (though no more likely to do so routinely). (Detailed results are summarized in table 32, Appendix 1.)

Other Postwriting Activities

Table 25 summarizes teachers' reports of their use of several other postwriting activities. The most obvious feature of the results is that little use is made of any of the alternative means of providing students with feedback about their work. Conferences with individual students were reported in regular use by 21 percent of those at grade eleven; even English teachers found time for such conferences in less than a quarter of their classrooms. Providing class time for students to read one another's work, duplicating papers so that everyone could have copies, and publishing in school or class publications were used regularly by no more than 13 percent of the teachers, though English (and to some extent business) teachers were more likely to make use of these techniques than were teachers of other subjects.

Again, uses of these postwriting activities were related to teachers' purposes in assigning writing. Teachers stressing subject-area information, as well as those stressing application of concepts, were significantly less likely to arrange individual conferences or to provide class time for students to read one another's work. Those stressing information were also significantly less likely to find outlets for student writing in school or class publications. (See table 31, Appendix 1.)

Though their teachers infrequently sought out broader audiences for student work, the students themselves often did. For their work in English, some 83 percent shared their work with others, most frequently their classmates but also their parents. Writing in the social sciences was less likely to be shared, but even there 48 percent of the students interviewed found broader audiences for their work, again centered on classmates and parents.

That the students seek out audiences for their work suggests they are proud of the writing they have done, that whatever the nature of the instructional situation that led to the writing, they became involved enough in what they were doing to want to share it. One of the English teachers at the city high school commented on the importance of such motivation, and noted in passing how she tied it together with sharing of work:

> Most of the motivation, I think, has to come from getting excited about the ideas in the material, or if they have no relevance for him, and they don't mean anything to him, why he doesn't have much success writing about them . . .
> And the more he knows, then, the more he likes to write and then I will say to students when I hand back a group of papers or

Table 25

Teaching Techniques: Postwriting

| Technique | Percent of Teachers Using Regularly[1] | | | | | | | | Chi-square tests[2] | |
| | Subject Area | | | | | | Grade | | | |
	English n=140	Foreign Language n=70	Math n=18	Science n=88	Social Science n=99	Business n=56	Ninth n=224	Eleventh n=236	Subject df=10	Grade df=2
Individual conferences	24.3	18.6	0.0	10.2	11.1	16.1	12.1	21.2	36.49***	6.88*
Class time for students to read each others papers	26.4	10.0	0.0	3.4	7.1	10.7	13.4	13.1	84.33***	5.92
Duplicate papers	10.0	7.1	11.1	11.4	13.1	14.3	12.1	11.9	14.82	6.01*
Publish papers	5.7	2.9	0.0[3]	0.0	1.0	7.1	2.7	3.8[4]	71.46***	0.93

Multivariate Analysis of Variance[5]

Effect	Lambda	df	F-Statistic
Subject	.45	55; 2003	6.79***
Grade	.93	11; 432	2.87**
Interaction	.86	55; 2003	1.19

1. Includes only teachers who assign writing of at least paragraph length.
2. Chi-square tests are based on three-point scales: never, sometimes, regularly.
3. n=19   4. n=237
5. The multivariate analysis is based on the full set of teaching techniques, tables 22, 23, and 25.
* $p < .05$; ** $p < .01$; *** $p < .001$

> a particular assignment, now, these five or six people did these papers, they are all A and B papers. Why don't you ask them if you can read them and compare their efforts with yours? That works beautifully, I think, too.

A more formal method of involving students with one another's papers involves peer evaluation, but as another English teacher noted, students can be very critical readers:

> I always used to have at least one paper graded by the peer group. I've always had that, because I think that's good. The basic thing you would find is they'd say, I can't read this. Well then, how am I supposed to read it? . . . they are more picky. I think they are more picky on a student's paper. They come for a lot of help. They are more picky than I am about the details in a paper.

Here, of course, the emphasis (as in the teacher's own responses) is on evaluating the student's work, rather than sharing it or working to improve it as an editor or a colleague might.

Summary

This chapter considered the instructional techniques that teachers use when they assign writing, grouping the techniques according to the stage of the writing process with which they are associated.

Prewriting activities were limited. In a typical writing situation, just over three minutes elapsed from the time the teacher began to pass out or discuss the assignment until students began to write. This was in part because much of the writing focused on information presented in lessons or textbooks; it was essentially a test of what the student had learned. In most cases students received explicit guidelines only about the length of the paper; there was little discussion of approaches to the topic or of what information should be included in the response. In the majority of the classrooms reported on, however, the students did begin their writing assignments in class, so they could ask questions about what was expected.

If prewriting activities were limited, those designed to help students while they were writing were almost nonexistent. About a third of the teachers simplified the writing tasks by breaking assignments into stages that could be completed one at a time. Just under 30 percent asked for more than one draft of required writing; most accepted the first draft handed in as the final one. Again, this may be because so many of the assignments function as tests of subject-area knowledge rather than as explorations of new material.

The major vehicle for writing instruction, in all subject areas, was the teacher's comments and corrections of completed work. Errors in writing mechanics were the most common focus of these responses; comments concerned with the ideas the student was expressing were the least frequently reported.

Within these general patterns, there were significant subject-area differences in the techniques used at each stage of the writing process. In general, teachers of English (and to a lesser extent teachers of business education and foreign languages) were more likely to provide help with the writing task, while teachers of science, social science, and math were more likely to be concerned with the accuracy of the information and the soundness of the conclusions.

Grade level differences were also apparent, though their magnitude was not so great. In general, ninth graders were given somewhat more help with their writing, and were less likely to be held strictly accountable for the accuracy of their work.

6 Synopsis of the Study

Design

The study was designed to (1) describe the writing secondary school students are asked to do in six major subject areas, (2) examine teachers' purposes and techniques in making writing assignments, and (3) illustrate the extent to which the characteristics of these assignments varied with subject area, grade level, and patterns of instruction.

The first phase of the study involved 259 observations of ninth and eleventh grade classes in two schools. These were selected randomly over the course of an academic year. Observers recorded the frequency and nature of student writing in the various subject areas, as well as the patterns of instruction surrounding such writing. Teacher and student attitudes toward writing were also studied, using standardized interview schedules.

In the second phase of the study, a stratified national sample of secondary school teachers reported on their attitudes toward writing, writing tasks assigned, and related instructional activities. The survey questionnaire was designed to make it possible to relate the findings from the intensively studied schools to patterns of instruction in schools nationally.

The Writing Students Do

Observational Study

1. Using a broad definition of writing, an average of 44 percent of the observed lesson time involved writing activities, with mechanical uses of writing (such as short-answer and fill-in-the-blank tasks) occurring 24 percent of the observed time, note-taking 17 percent, and writing of paragraph length or longer occurring 3 percent of the observed time. Similarly, homework assignments involved writing of at least paragraph length 3 percent of the time.

2. Writing-related activities were used most often in mathematics, science, and social science classes, where they primarily involved calculations, short-answer responses to study sheets, and fill-in-the-blank and multiple-choice exercises.

3. Writing of at least paragraph length occurred most frequently in English classes (averaging 10 percent of lesson time).

4. Note-taking was observed most often (39 percent of the time) in social science classes and least often (less than 6 percent of the time) in foreign language classes.

5. Information from student interviews revealed that informational uses of writing, including note-taking, were the most prevalent tasks assigned and that imaginative uses of writing were limited for the most part to English classes—and even there were reported by less than half of the students.

National Survey

1. In the national survey, teachers in all subject areas surveyed indicated that they made frequent use of at least some writing-related activities; these activities were dominated by note-taking and short-answer responses.

2. Writing of at least paragraph length was reported as a frequent activity for tests, homework, or classwork in 27 percent of the classes at grade nine and 36 percent at grade eleven. English classes were the most likely to require such writing.

3. Of the writing samples supplied by the surveyed teachers, 85 percent reflected informational uses of writing. This was virtually the only type of writing in science classes (where it represented 99 percent of the sample); in English classes it represented about three-quarters of the papers.

4. Both teachers' reports and analysis of the writing samples indicated that the level of abstraction in informational writing increases in the upper grades.

Audiences for Student Work

1. In the observational study, too few writing episodes were observed to draw useful conclusions about similarities or differences between grade levels and subject areas.

2. In the national survey, the teacher in the role of examiner was the prime audience for student writing in all subject areas. Only 10 percent of the teachers reported that student writing was regularly read by other students. A slightly higher proportion reported some use of writing that was read only by the student, with such uses concentrated in mathematics, science, and social studies classes.

3. Of the writing samples submitted by surveyed teachers, 88 percent were addressed to the teacher as the primary audience. A third of the papers

seemed to have been written as part of a teacher-learner dialogue rather than a display of completed learning.

4. Writing as part of such a teacher-learner dialogue was more likely to occur in English and social science classes than in science or business education classes.

5. The most frequent writing task represented in the samples of school writing was analysis directed to the teacher as examiner, which accounted for 22 percent of all the writing collected. More generally, 48 percent of the sample was informational writing to the teacher as examiner.

Length of Writing Assignments

1. The typical assignment reported by surveyed teachers included a page or less of writing. However, 47 percent of the English teachers and 20 percent or more of the science and social science teachers reported typically assigning up to two pages.

2. Longer assignments were made occasionally in all subjects, but particularly in English and the social sciences.

Purposes for Assigning Writing

Teachers' Attitudes

1. Two major dimensions were found to underlie the reasons that teachers in the national survey asked students to write. The first dimension reflected the extent to which the teacher used writing to foster learning of subject-area information versus to explore the personal or imaginative experiences of the students. The second dimension contrasted teachers who stressed the application of subject-area concepts with those who stressed development of students' writing skills.

2. In the national sample as a whole, 70 percent of the teachers emphasized subject-area information in their writing assignments; 16 percent were primarily concerned with personal experience. Similarly, 44 percent stressed subject-area concepts, contrasted with 24 percent who stressed the development of writing skills.

3. In general, English teachers were more likely to stress personal and imaginative experience, while math and science teachers were more concerned with a combination of subject-area information and the application of concepts in new situations.

4. Business education and social science teachers, as groups, placed some emphasis on subject-area knowledge and relatively equal stress on writing skills and the application of concepts.

The Writing Students Do, Revisited

1. Writing of at least paragraph length was assigned frequently by 73 percent of the teachers who stressed personal experience, contrasted with 18 percent of those who stressed subject-area information.

2. Similarly, writing of at least paragraph length was assigned frequently by 48 percent of those whose assignments stressed writing skills, compared with only 16 percent of the teachers who stressed application of subject-area concepts.

3. Whatever their specific views about the purposes of assigning writing, teachers in all groups emphasized informational writing. Within this general pattern, the assignments made by teachers concerned with the application of concepts involved writing at a higher level of abstraction.

4. Personal and imaginative writing were at least twice as likely to be assigned by teachers who stressed individual experience rather than subject-area information, and by teachers who stressed writing skills rather than the application of concepts. These same teachers were also more likely to provide wider audiences for student work, rather than simply reading and marking the papers themselves.

5. Some 82 percent of the teachers surveyed felt that both the subject-area teacher and the English teacher were responsible for the development of student writing skills. Teachers who stressed subject-area information, as well as those who stressed the application of concepts, were less likely to accept this responsibility.

Writing Instruction

Prewriting

1. In the observational studies, the time that elapsed from the point at which the teacher began an assignment until students were expected to begin to write averaged just over three minutes.

2. Two-thirds of student reports on prewriting activities noted instructions related to form (length and layout of the paper). Other sorts of instructions were rare. Specific hints as to the appropriate content were reported over 25 percent of the time, teacher-supplied outlines were reported over 10 percent of the time, and there was occasional discussion of the topic or of model responses. In general, student responses were similar to the observers' findings.

3. In the national survey, the most popular technique in helping students get started was to have them begin their writing in class, so that they

could ask questions about what was expected if they found themselves in difficulties. This approach was most popular with English teachers, nearly 80 percent of whom reported that they regularly assign writing in this way; it was least likely to be used regularly by math and science teachers (11 and 33 percent, respectively).

4. Model responses for students to examine were used in 29 percent of the classes. They were cited most frequently by foreign language teachers, least frequently by science teachers. About a third of the English teachers reported regular use of writing models.

5. Brainstorming was reported in regular use by some 37 percent of the English teachers and by no more than 14 percent in any other subject area.

Writing and Revising

1. In the national survey, nearly three-quarters of the English teachers and half of the business education and foreign language teachers reported regular inclass writing, compared with 25 percent or fewer of the science, social studies, and mathematics teachers. One of the most frequent contexts for inclass writing, however, was the essay exam.

2. Some 29 percent of the teachers reported "regularly" asking students to write more than one draft. This was most likely in English classes (59 percent), least likely in science (7 percent).

3. Use of successive drafts for more than minor editorial changes required help from the teacher for the majority of the students interviewed. In writing for English, only 23 percent claimed to make changes that went beyond spelling, mechanics, usage, or vocabulary choice; in writing for social studies, one third claimed to make such larger changes.

Postwriting

1. The most frequent response to student work was to mark errors in writing mechanics; this was done routinely by 71 percent of the teachers surveyed, and was also rated as one of the most important responses by 47 percent.

2. Responses that directly engaged the ideas that the student was expressing were given routinely by less than a fifth of the teachers.

3. Conferences with individual students about their writing were reported in regular use by 12 percent of the teachers at grade nine and 21 percent at grade eleven. English teachers reported regular conferences in 24 percent of their classes; math teachers did not use them regularly in any of the classes on which they reported.

4. Teachers stressing subject-area information or the application of concepts were less likely to arrange individual conferences or to provide time for students to read one another's work.

5. Some 83 percent of the students reported sharing their work in English with others, most frequently with their classmates but also with their parents. Writing in the social sciences was less likely to be shared, but even there 48 percent of the students interviewed found broader audiences for their work, again centered on classmates and parents.

7 Improving the Teaching of Writing

Our study of writing in the secondary school has produced a wealth of information about teacher attitudes and practices related to the teaching of writing in the major subject areas of the secondary school. The detailed findings have been presented in the previous chapters, with brief summaries at the end of each chapter and a final recapitulation in chapter 6. The longer-range goal of our work, however, is not just to describe what is happening, but to deepen our understanding of the processes involved so that we can suggest directions for improvement—or at least fruitful avenues for future research. In this final chapter, we will hazard some of these interpretations.

Writing Tasks

It has become a commonplace to say that in order to learn to write better, students should be asked to write more often. In one sense the present work supports this notion. In the observational studies, students were spending only 3 percent of their class time working on essays or other writing of at least paragraph length, and in the national survey 32 percent of the teachers said that they *never* assigned such writing to the students in the class on which they were reporting. Only 31 percent reported *frequently* using such writing tasks. (As a national figure, this probably overestimates the extent to which writing is used, since the teachers were nominated as "good" teachers by their principals, specifically to participate in a study of writing.)

On the other hand, students were engaged in a variety of related activities using written language to record information for later reference by the teacher, themselves, or their fellow students. These activities included such things as multiple-choice and fill-in-the-blank exercises, math calculations, and short-answer responses requiring only a sentence or two. Analyzed as writing activities, such tasks are characterized by a separation of the problem of constructing coherent text in language appropriate to the subject area from the problem of remembering subject-area information and concepts. Essentially, the teacher takes over all of the difficulties inherent in using language appropriate to a subject area—including much of the specialized vocabulary and rules of procedure which are embedded in the text—and leaves the student only the task of mechanically "slotting-in" the missing information.

Such mechanical writing activities, as most teachers know, are highly efficient for some purposes, particularly for testing how well a student has learned specific content or skills. Too frequently, however, teachers seem not to realize that the part of the task which they have taken over also involves important skills that are as relevant to the students' subject-area learning as to their writing instruction. Language is used differently in the various academic disciplines: vocabularies are specialized, forms of argument and organization are conventionalized, and the typical modes of discourse vary. (We have seen some of this in the subject-area differences in preferred types of writing; these do not polarize into English versus the rest of the curriculum but show characteristic discipline-by-discipline patterns.) To fully understand a science, a student must learn to write within the conventions of the discipline—but too frequently it is only in English class (and there only in the context of literary criticism) that we provide the opportunity for students to write much at all.

Becoming comfortable in the conventions of specialized disciplines is one justification for a shift in the balance of writing exercises away from the present reliance on easily graded mechanical tasks toward more extensive writing. The other and probably more powerful justification has to do with writing as a tool for exploring a subject. When the task for the student is limited to supplying relatively isolated items of information, or to applying new concepts in the context of highly structured exercises, the knowledge called for can remain isolated and detached. There is little need to relate the knowledge to other aspects of the students' experience, nor even to integrate the various learnings within a single subject area. It is only when students begin to write on their own that the implications of new knowledge begin to be worked through and (as some of the teachers in our study pointed out) that they really come to know the material.

This is because writing can be a powerful process for discovering meaning rather than just transcribing an idea that is in some sense waiting fully developed in the writer's mind. Our language provides a whole panoply of devices that not only convey our meaning to others, but help us develop the meaning for ourselves. These devices take many shapes: they include the *buts* and the *ands* and the *althoughs* that relate one set of information to another; they include the basic syntactic relationships of subjects and objects and predicates; and they include structural devices that underlie larger stretches of discourse—time sequence in narrative, or generalization and supporting detail in exposition.

In our concern with writing as a way to express an idea or reveal subject-area knowledge, we tend to overlook the extent to which these devices help us generate new ideas "at the point of utterance." This is perhaps clearer if we think of a complex algebraic problem. All the terms of the problem are present in our mind, but it is not until we set them down on paper and carry through the steps that most of us can reach an answer. Writing about a complex or unfamiliar question is very similar, though the devices for working out the meaning are linguistic rather than mathematical.

One of the major problems with an overemphasis on mechanical writing tasks is that the students may never learn to use such resources as their own, relying instead upon the structure or scaffold that the teacher has provided.

Unfortunately, even in those contexts where students were being asked to write at some length, the writing was often used merely as a vehicle to test knowledge of specific content, with the teacher functioning primarily in the role of examiner. Although this too is a legitimate use of writing, its relationship to the development of writing skills must be at best tenuous. As we have seen, the teacher as examiner can be a very undemanding audience, one willing to interpret what the student meant to say. Teachers are able to do this in large part because they already know what should have been said and are looking for hints that at least some of the desired material is present. There is a similarity here with the mechanical writing tasks: the text-forming aspect of the task has been minimized in favor of the information that must be cited. And as the text is minimized, so too is the opportunity to use the language resources embedded in that text to more fully explore new ideas.

Because the emphasis is on specific items of information, rather than on the way those items are integrated and presented in coherent prose, such writing situations provide little opportunity for instruction that might help students develop specific writing skills. For learning to write well, the most effective writing situation will be one in which the effectiveness of the writing matters— where the student can savor the success of having presented a convincing argument or struggle with the problems of having failed to do so. In such situations the teacher can sometimes intervene directly, helping students develop their writing skills by demonstrating the effects of different methods of organization and presentation. If all that really matters, however, is that the right items of information be cited, then the development of such new writing skills will be essentially irrelevant, and they will be ignored by student and teacher alike.

As a first step in improving the writing of secondary school students, then, we need more situations in which writing can serve as a tool for learning rather than as a means to display acquired knowledge. Bringing this about will take further work in two dimensions: (1) practical descriptions of specific techniques and activities that can be successfully incorporated into the various content areas (including English)—descriptions of "good practice" that will make sense to the subject-area teachers involved; (2) systematic investigation of the benefits of such activities, in terms both of student writing skills and of subject-area knowledge. The research base currently available to teachers of writing does little to demonstrate these benefits, but we believe that they can be shown to be real and powerful.

Instructional Practices

The most obvious finding to emerge from looking at the instructional techniques adopted to help students with their writing is that very few such techniques are used at all. To some extent this is a function of the fact that so
much of the writing students do is assigned in a test situation, rather than an
instructional one. To some extent, too, it comes from a conceptualization of
writing as a simple skill which a given student has or does not have. There is
little reflection in the practices we observed of recent studies of composing
which suggest that writing is a process with a number of distinct stages, each
with its own focus and demands (Emig, 1971; Graves, 1975; Perl, 1979). In
the simplest formulation, the stages include prewriting, writing, and editing.

Prewriting is the time during which information is gathered and ideas played
with. It may include reading, talking, and simply thinking about a topic. Sometimes it includes an incubation period when initial thoughts are set aside and
allowed to coalesce without conscious attention. In real life situations, this
stage can extend for weeks or months. Yet in the classrooms observed, only
three minutes elapsed from the time the teacher began explaining a writing
topic until the time students were expected to begin to write. Discussion of
the topic was rare; it usually took the form of teacher questions prompting
brief student response. Rare too was any gathering and sorting of relevant
information, whether through procedures such as brainstorming or through
systematic reference work. Indeed, most writing assignments began with the
expectation that the student already knew what to say and could rapidly begin
to write.

The *writing* stage of the composing process is the time when the topic is
developed on paper. Getting started on the writing stage is often difficult and
painful, producing many false starts and discarded openings. At this stage the
concern is with the ideas the writer wants to express, with laying out an argument and its implications, or with the basic scenes and storyline in fiction. Not
infrequently, these ideas will change in the process of writing about them.
Successive drafts will be needed before the various sections of the writing will
be fully consonant and supportive of one another.

Again, there is little in current practice that parallels this model of composing. The time span devoted to the writing—like that devoted to prewriting
activities—is typically short, beginning part way through a lesson with time
"to finish up" at home. Students are rarely asked to write more than one draft,
and this first-and-final draft is often surrounded by demands for mechanical
accuracy, neatness, and organization. Major revision is frustrated not just by the
time constraints, but by the almost universally negative reaction to "messy"
papers.

The third stage described in studies of the writing process is that of *editing*, polishing what has been written to share with a wider audience. This is the stage for attention to mechanical errors, spelling, punctuation, usage, handwriting. It can also be a stage for fine-tuning for a particular audience or to achieve a particular tone. In professional writing, this stage involves the work of an editor, who brings a detachment which is hard to obtain when looking at one's own writing, and whose contributions to the final published piece, though usually unsung, can be very substantial.

In current practice, this may be the stage of writing that is stressed most, though the purpose gets distorted in the process. In natural writing situations, editing is totally motivated by the fact that the writing is to be shared; the editorial changes are in the service of a polished final manuscript, not private criticisms for the author to read and file away. Teachers' comments on student papers are in many ways parallel to those of an editor, and it is not unusual for English classes to be taught some of the standard proofreading symbols. But in the classroom, the edited writing is not ordinarily about to be revised; it is simply evaluated for the writer's benefit, to be filed away rather than shared with others. However detailed and constructive a teacher's comments may be, their effectiveness depends upon the extent to which the students read the comments and upon whether simply reading them is enough to teach a student how to correct the errors. Since students rarely are asked to write another draft they have few chances to learn how to use an editor's suggestions and revisions to produce a better manuscript.

The composing process probably differs depending upon the type of writing involved, the age and ability of the writer, and the familiarity of the material being written about. But even given this variability, the recognition that the writing process has distinct stages provides a useful—and underutilized—perspective in examining classroom practice. Too often, school tasks are structured so that a concern with mechanical correctness interferes with the writing stage, when there are other and more difficult tasks. Similarly, we short-circuit the brainstorming and discussion needed in prewriting, insisting that students "get down to work." And we demand neat and tidy first drafts that allow little room for the students to discover new ideas as they write—ideas which when developed further usually require that earlier parts of an essay be discarded and reworked.

As a second step, then, in the improvement of writing instruction, we need to bring recent work on the nature of the composing process to the attention of a broader spectrum of teachers to provide them with a framework for analyzing the contexts within which they ask their students to write. At the same time, we need to test hypotheses about the ways specific instructional techniques will interact with the various stages of the writing process.

The Good, the Better, and the Best

The focus of the present study was descriptive, and the instruments and observational procedures were nonevaluative. Yet the staff of the study are themselves experienced teachers, and in the course of some 300 classroom visits we developed strong impressions about the nature of the teaching and learning that were taking place. During the course of the year we saw much good teaching. Inevitably, we saw some lessons where the chemistry was wrong and it seemed that little if any learning was taking place. For our present purposes the lessons that failed completely are of little interest; of more concern are the differences between lessons that gave the impression of a pleasant and effective teaching situation, and those in which that pleasant atmosphere of competence was transformed into something more exciting. After studying and summarizing their logs and records, the observers abstracted the following characteristics from 114 "good" to "best" lessons.

Good Lesson

> there is an ordered variety of tasks for students to perform
>
> assignments are clear and their purpose evident
>
> students perform teacher-designated tasks
>
> grades are used as the primary motivation
>
> when assigned, writing is used as a measure of student knowledge or performance
>
> the predominant teaching technique is teacher-led class discussion

Better Lesson

> students are actively involved in teacher-designed tasks
>
> the teacher maintains a high level of student interest
>
> the teacher encourages a free flow of give and take
>
> the teacher incorporates student experiences into the lesson
>
> the predominant teaching technique is teacher-led class discussion—but student-led discussions are encouraged
>
> students are prepared for writing assignments with prewriting activities such as audiovisual presentations or modelling
>
> there is a climate of trust between teacher and students

Best Lesson

> students assume an active role in their own learning

the teacher encourages students to explore and discover and seldom dominates the class

students' own experiences are freely incorporated into class discussions

students are enthusiastic about their work

writing is viewed as a means of learning and emerges naturally out of other activities

In all of the lessons described here, an atmosphere of mutual trust and collaboration had been established. Students and teachers were working together toward similar ends, with minimal conflict or resistance. For the most part, they seemed to like one another. What seemed to distinguish the outstanding classes from the others observed was the nature of the three-way relationship between the teacher, the task, and the student. In the good lessons, the teacher served essentially as a transmitter of knowledge or skill, a wise master of the subject area imparting that knowledge to a new set of disciples. The tasks set were thus relatively closed; student responses were primarily an attempt to discover the answer that the teacher wanted.

In the better lessons, and even more so in the few that were really exceptional, the students were faced with problems that had to be solved out of their own intellectual and experiential resources. Often they would work together to solve problems posed by the teacher; this forced the students both to articulate their solutions more clearly and to defend them in the face of opposing opinions. The subject of the discussion seemed less important than the openness of the approach; what mattered was the sense that the students could offer legitimate solutions of their own rather than discover a solution the teacher had already devised. Thus the topics of such lessons ranged broadly, from an attempt to reach consensus on an interpretation of Thoreau's *Civil Disobedience* to an explanation of the principles involved in an angular momentum to a discussion of whether abortion should be legalized. When writing assignments followed such lessons, they were treated by the students as a way to continue an activity in which they had become deeply involved.

The context for student writing provided by these lessons is a natural one, where the writing is motivated by a need to communicate and valued as an expression of something the writer wants to say. Contrasted with the writing to display knowledge characteristic of the good lessons, it is also more difficult: the writer has to organize and communicate opinions to a reader who does not already know what is going to be said, and who may well hold an opposing opinion.

Creating contexts in which writing serves such natural purposes, then, is our third suggestion for improving the teaching of writing; it is also probably the most difficult to implement. The good and best lessons differ not just in the enthusiasm they provoked in our observers; they also reflect differing philosophies of education, each with long traditions. The best hope of reconciling these traditions is to understand their classroom implications more thoroughly. Certainly in suggesting a shift in emphasis away from writing to display information toward writing to fulfill other communicative functions, we believe that these contexts will foster and support the learning of information and skills that is also needed. Investigating that hypothesis is the next research task.

References

Applebee, Arthur N. (1978a). *A Survey of Teaching Conditions in English, 1977.* Urbana, Ill.: National Council of Teachers of English.

Applebee, Arthur N. (1978b). Teaching High-Achieving Students: A Survey of Winners of the 1977 NCTE Achievement Awards in Writing. *Research in the Teaching of English* 12:4, 339–348.

Applebee, Arthur N., Fran Lehr, and Anne Auten. (1980). *A Study of Writing in the Secondary School.* Final Report NIE–G–79–0174. ERIC Document no. ED 197 347.

Barnes, Douglas. (1976). *From Communication to Curriculum.* Harmondsworth, England: Penguin Books.

Barnes, Douglas, and Denis Shemilt. (1974). Transmission and Interpretation. *Educational Review* 26:3, 213–228.

Bereiter, Carl, and Marlene Scardamalia. (in press). From Conversation to Composition: The Role of Instruction in Developmental Process. In R. Glazer (ed.), *Advances in Instructional Psychology,* Vol. 2. Hillsdale, N.J.: Erlbaum.

Bracewell, Robert J., Marlene Scardamalia, and Carl Bereiter. (1978). The Development of Audience Awareness in Writing. Toronto, Canada. ERIC Document no. ED 154 433.

Britton, James. (1970). *Language and Learning.* London: Allen Lane, The Penguin Press.

Britton, James, Tony Burgess, Nancy Martin, Alex McLeod, and Harold Rosen. (1975). *The Development of Writing Abilities (11-18).* London: Macmillan Education Ltd. for the Schools Council.

Bruner, Jerome S. (1978). The Role of Dialogue in Language Acquisition. In A. Sinclair et al. (eds.) *The Child's Conception of Language.* New York: Springer-Verlag.

Bureau of the Census. (1978). *Census Geography.* Data Access Descriptions No. 33. Washington, D.C.: U.S. Department of Commerce.

Cazden, Courtney. (1980). Peekaboo as an Instructional Model: Discourse Development at Home and at School. *Papers and Reports of Child Language Development, Vol. 17,* 1–29.

Cooper, Charles, and Lee Odell. (1977). *Evaluating Writing: Describing, Measuring, Judging.* Urbana, Ill.: National Council of Teachers of English.

Crowhurst, Marion, and Gene L. Piche. (1979). Audience and Mode of Discourse Effects on Syntactic Complexity in Writing at Two Grade Levels. *Research in the Teaching of English* 13:2, 101–109.

Donlan, Dan. (1974). Teaching Writing in the Content Areas: Eleven Hypotheses from a Teacher Survey. *Research in the Teaching of English* 8:2, 250–262.

Eco, Umberto. (1979). *The Role of the Reader: Explorations on the Semiotics of Texts.* Bloomington: Indiana University Press.

Emig, Janet. (1971). *The Composing Processes of Twelfth Graders.* Research Report No. 13. Urbana, Ill.: National Council of Teachers of English.

Florio, Susan. (1978). *The Problem of Dead Letters: Social Perspectives on the Teaching of Writing.* Research Series No. 34. East Lansing: Michigan State University Institute for Research on Teaching. ERIC Document no. ED 163 492.

Freedle, Roy O. (ed.). (1979). *New Directions in Discourse Processing.* Norwood, N.J.: ABLEX Publishing Company.

Graves, Donald. (1973). Children's Writing. Ph.D. dissertation, State University of New York at Buffalo.

Graves, Donald. (1975). An Examination of the Writing Processes of Seven Year Old Children. *Research in the Teaching of English* 9:3, 227–241.

Halliday, M. A. K., (1977). *Learning How to Mean: Explorations in the Development of Language.* New York: Elsevier.

Halliday, M. A. K., and Rugaiya Hasan. (1976). *Cohesion in English.* London: Longman Group, Ltd.

Holsti, O. R. (1969). *Content Analysis for the Social Sciences and Humanities.* New York: Addison Wesley.

Kinneavy, James L. (1971). *A Theory of Discourse.* Englewood Cliffs, N.J.: Prentice-Hall.

Kuhn, Thomas S. (1962). *The Structure of Scientific Revolutions. Second Edition. enlarged. International Encyclopedia of Unified Sciences, Volume 2, Number 2.* Chicago and London: The University of Chicago Press, 1970 edition.

Lunzer, Eric, and Keith Gardner. (1979). *The Effective Use of Reading.* London: Heinemann Educational Books.

Martin, Nancy, Pat D'Arcy, Bryan Newton, and Robert Parker. (1976). *Writing and Learning Across the Curriculum 11–6.* London: Ward Lock Educational.

Mead, George Herbert. (1934). *Mind, Self, and Society.* Chicago, Ill.: The University of Chicago Press.

Metzger, Elizabeth. (1976). An Instrument for Describing Written Products. Learning Center, State University of New York at Buffalo. ERIC Document no. ED 133 749.

Moffett, James. (1968). *Teaching the Universe of Discourse.* Boston: Houghton Mifflin. ERIC Document no. ED 030 664.

National Assessment of Educational Progress. (1975). *Writing Mechanics, 1969–1974.* Denver, Colo.: Education Commission of the States.

National Assessment of Educational Progress. (1976). *Expressive Writing.* Denver, Colo.: Education Commission of the States.

National Assessment of Educational Progress. (1977a). *Explanatory and Persuasive Letter Writing.* Denver, Colo.: Education Commission of the States.

National Assessment of Educational Progress. (1977b). *Write/Rewrite: An Assessment of Revision Skills.* Denver, Colo.: Education Commission of the States.

National Assessment of Educational Progress. (1980a). *Writing Achievement, 1969-79: Results from the Third National Writing Assessment, Vol. I—17 Year Olds.* Denver, Colo.: Education Commission of the States.

National Assessment of Educational Progress. (1980b). *Writing Achievement, 1969-79: Results from the Third National Writing Assessment, Vol. II—13 Year Olds.* Denver, Colo.: Education Commission of the States.

National Assessment of Educational Progress. (1980c). *Writing Achievement, 1969-79: Results from the Third National Writing Assessment, Vol. III—9 Year Olds.* Denver, Colo.: Education Commission of the States.

Olson, David R. (1977). From Utterance to Text: The Bias of Language in Speech and Writing. *Harvard Educational Review* 47:3, 257-281.

Perl, Sondra. (1979). The Composing Processes of Unskilled College Writers. *Research in the Teaching of English* 13:4, 317-336.

Perron, John D. (1977). Written Syntactic Complexity and the Modes of Discourse. University of Georgia. ERIC Document no. ED 139 009.

Renehan, William. (1977). *Seven-Year-Olds: Talking and Writing.* Victoria: Australian Council for Educational Research.

Rubin, Donald L., and Gene L. Piche. (1979). Development of Syntactic and Strategic Aspects of Audience Adaptation Skills in Written Persuasive Communication. *Research in the Teaching of English* 13:4, 293-316.

Searle, Dennis James. (1975). A Study of the Classroom Language Activity of Five Selected High School Students. *Research in the Teaching of English* 9:4, 267-286.

Squire, James R., and Roger K. Applebee. (1968). *High School English Instruction Today.* New York: Appleton-Century-Croft.

Tate, Gary, (ed.). (1976). *Teaching Composition: 10 Bibliographic Essays.* Fort Worth: Texas Christian University Press.

Whale, Kathleen B., and Sam Robinson. (1978). Modes of Students' Writings: A Descriptive Study. *Research in the Teaching of English* 12:4, 349-355.

Appendix 1: Supplementary Tables

Table 26

Profiles of Class Activities: Laboratory School

	English		Foreign Language		Math		Science		Social Science	
					Mean Percent of Time					
Activity	Grd 9 n=9	Grd 11 n=9	Grd 9 n=8	Grd 11 n=11	Grd 9 n=10	Grd 11 n=8	Grd 9 n=10	Grd 11 n=9	Grd 9 n=10	Grd 11 n=9
Administration and Transition	19.6	10.8	8.7	13.2	9.1	10.5	14.3	10.8	9.2	32.4
Teacher presentation	0.2	0.0	0.0	5.2	0.6	0.0	6.9	9.0	15.8	12.2
Student presentation	0.0	8.3	3.8	0.4	3.0	1.5	1.4	2.9	0.0	0.6
Class discussion (teacher-led)	30.2	36.1	34.0	49.3	37.8	53.6	15.7	43.6	58.0	54.8
Class discussion (pupil-led)	0.0	0.0	4.3	0.0	0.4	0.5	6.8	11.4	0.0	0.0
Group work	22.7	14.3	2.3	0.0	0.0	0.0	24.7	11.1	7.5	0.0
Individual work	12.1	20.4	10.5	6.2	24.3	30.0	0.0	7.1	0.0	0.0
Correction of exercises	7.7	1.3	6.8	17.0	12.8	2.8	0.9	4.2	0.0	0.0
Test taking	9.9	8.7	27.0	6.0	13.0	1.3	19.5	0.0	9.6	0.0
Other	0.0	0.0	4.3	1.2	0.0	0.0	8.7	0.0	0.0	0.0

n=93 lessons

Table 27

Profiles of Class Activities: City High School

	Mean Percent of Time																
	English		Foreign Language		Math		Science		Social Science		Business Education	Special Education		Other			
Activity	Grd 9 n=16	Grd 11 n=22	Grd 9 n=11	Grd 11 n=6	Grd 9 n=12	Grd 11 n=7	Grd 9 n=8	Grd 11 n=11	Grd 9 n=10	Grd 11 n=9	Grd 11 n=17	Grd 9 n=5	Grd 11 n=9	Grd 9 n=5	Grd 11 n=18
Administration and Transition	15.7	15.3	22.2	17.1	13.3	9.9	14.6	11.6	22.4	12.9	14.5	12.8	10.7	4.0	14.9
Teacher presentation	2.9	4.8	8.9	10.3	0.0	2.6	16.9	9.3	5.8	13.7	7.8	12.0	0.0	7.6	14.9
Student presentation	0.0	1.7	0.4	4.3	0.7	0.0	0.0	0.0	0.0	0.0	0.0	0.0	0.0	0.0	0.0
Class discussion (teacher-led)	22.4	27.6	48.9	41.7	26.7	37.3	49.6	20.0	16.0	27.8	25.5	23.6	40.4	0.0	23.4
Class discussion (pupil-led)	0.0	0.0	0.0	0.0	0.0	0.0	0.0	2.6	0.0	0.0	0.0	0.0	0.0	0.0	0.0
Group work	0.0	10.7	0.0	1.3	4.3	0.0	6.5	16.5	0.0	0.0	0.0	0.0	0.0	0.0	5.8
Individual work	34.1	32.9	4.0	3.7	36.5	14.2	9.9	28.2	29.4	34.3	39.7	51.6	39.2	88.4	27.4
Correction of exercises	10.0	1.0	12.1	2.3	16.5	28.7	2.5	5.3	10.0	6.0	4.7	0.0	0.9	0.0	8.9
Test taking	16.3	4.1	0.5	19.3	0.0	7.3	0.0	6.5	16.4	5.2	7.8	0.0	6.9	0.0	4.7
Other	0.1	0.5	0.0	0.0	2.0	0.0	0.0	0.0	0.0	0.0	0.0	0.0	0.0	0.0	0.0

n=166 lessons

Table 28

Percent of Lesson Time Involving Writing Activities

Activity	Mean Percent of Time														
	English		Foreign Language		Math		Science		Social Science		Business Education	Special Education		Other	
	Grd 9	Grd 11	Grd 9	Grd 11	Grd 9	Grd 11	Grd 9	Grd 11	Grd 9	Grd 11	Grd 11	Grd 9	Grd 11	Grd 9	Grd 11
Mechanical Uses															
Laboratory School	12.1	10.9	34.0	7.8	44.8	32.2	25.9	25.9	5.0	0.0	31.5	51.6	53.4	0.0	13.2
City High School	18.1	18.4	9.1	16.3	66.3	37.0	2.3	41.5	26.0	17.6	9.5				5.9
Informational Uses															
Note taking															
Laboratory School	2.4	19.2	6.1	7.8	16.2	21.3	22.2	24.3	65.0	42.7		0.0	0.0	0.0	
City High School	4.4	26.5	5.8	0.0	7.7	27.3	45.6	4.9	5.0	44.5			5.8		
Other															
Laboratory School	14.9	14.9	0.0	0.0	0.0	0.0	0.0	0.0	4.6	0.0		0.0		0.0	0.0
City High School	5.9	4.6	0.0	3.0	0.0	0.0	0.0	0.0	14.6	0.0	2.0				
Personal or Imaginative Uses															
Laboratory School	0.0	7.8	0.2	0.0	0.0	0.0	0.0	0.0	0.0	0.0		0.0	2.4	0.0	0.0
City High School	0.0	0.9	0.0	0.0	0.0	0.0	0.0	0.0	0.0	0.0	0.0				
Any Uses															
Laboratory School	29.5	52.7	40.4	15.6	61.0	53.6	48.2	50.2	74.6	42.7		51.6	61.6	0.0	19.1
City High School	28.4	50.4	14.9	19.3	73.9	64.3	47.8	46.4	45.6	62.1	43.0				
Number of Lessons															
Laboratory School	9	9	8	11	10	8	10	9	10	9		5	9	5	18
City High School	16	22	11	6	12	7	8	11	10	9	17				

Table 29

Relationships between Audience and Function in Student Writing

Audience	Percent of Total Sample								
	Record	Report	Summary	Analysis	Theory	Persuasive	Personal	Stories	Poems
Teacher, as part of teacher-learner dialogue	0.3	7.9	4.5	12.5	2.0	0.3	4.2	1.4	0.0
Teacher, as examiner	0.3	9.9	15.3	22.1	0.0	0.6	1.7	2.8	1.7
Wider audience	0.0	2.0	2.8	3.4	0.8	0.3	1.1	1.7	0.3
Number of papers	2	70	80	134	10	4	25	21	7

Table 30

Relationships between Purposes for Writing and Writing-Related Activities

Activity	Percent of Teachers Reporting Frequent Use						Chi-square test[1]	
	Stress on Information			Stress on Concepts				
	High n=520	Moderate n=101	Low n=120	High n=318	Moderate n=235	Low n=179	Information df=4	Concepts df=4
Multiple-choice or fill-in-the-blank	34.4	29.7	25.0	33.3	32.3	31.3	5.84	0.73
Note-taking	52.5	46.5	51.7	52.8	52.8	47.5	3.46	4.36
Copying, dictation, or translation	26.7	25.7	27.5	23.3	27.2	33.0	15.73**	6.87
Calculations	45.4	13.9	9.2	52.2	26.4	14.0	97.30***	93.22***
Short-answer	41.2	50.0[2]	55.0	43.7	44.5[3]	46.9	9.16	0.76
Proofs	19.2	2.9[2]	3.3	20.4	13.1[3]	5.0	49.19***	63.35***
Paragraph-length writing	17.9	58.4	63.3	16.0	38.3	48.0	154.49***	97.22***

1. Chi-square tests are based on three-point scales: not used, used occasionally, used frequently.
2. n=102
3. n=236

* p < .05; ** p < .01; p < .001

Table 31

Relationships between Purposes for Writing and Teaching Techniques

| Techniques | Percent of Teachers Using Regularly | | | | | | Chi-square test[1] | |
| | Stress on Information | | | Stress on Concepts | | | Information df=4 | Concepts df=4 |
	High n=278	Moderate n=87	Low n=107	High n=150	Moderate n=178	Low n=144		
Assignment sheet	34.5	28.7	37.4	37.3	30.9	34.7	2.13	3.27
Model responses	26.6	29.9	36.4	22.7	34.8	30.6	4.66	8.35
Beginning in class, to answer questions	43.5	59.8	68.2	43.3	54.5	59.0	26.53***	7.95
Write in class	37.1	52.9	66.4	36.0	46.1	58.3	42.16***	15.87**
Break assignments into steps	31.7	27.6	37.4	30.7	31.5	34.0	11.56*	1.34
Brainstorming	11.2	26.4	38.3	15.3	21.9	23.6	53.07***	11.67*
Require more than one draft	19.8	34.5	50.5	16.7	29.2	41.7	47.75***	39.45***
Individual conferences	12.9	19.5	23.4	12.7	18.5	18.8	16.98**	16.97**
Class time for students to read papers	5.4	17.2	29.9	8.7	16.9	13.9	56.55***	20.11***
Duplicate papers	11.9	11.5	12.1	10.0	14.0	11.1	1.17	5.09
Publish papers	2.2[2]	2.3	7.5	2.0[3]	5.6	2.1	34.78***	8.16

1. Chi-squares are based on three-point scales: never used, used sometimes, used regularly.
2. n=279
3. n=151

* p < .05; ** p < .01; *** p < .001

Table 32

Relationships between Purposes for Writing
and Responses to Student Writing

Responses	Percent of Teachers Indicating						Chi-square test	
	Stress on Information			Stress on Concepts			Information df=4	Concepts df=4
	High n=277	Moderate n=86	Low n=106	High n=148	Moderate n=179	Low n=143		
Important to[1]								
Indicate mechanical errors	45.8	51.2	52.8	25.0	45.8	75.5	5.57	97.69***
Suggest improvements in style	27.4	40.7	58.5	20.3	39.7	51.7	48.58***	48.26***
Point out errors of fact	54.2	27.9	21.7	57.4	41.9	25.9	46.96***	34.06***
Assess accuracy of conclusion	49.1	41.9	15.1	59.5	41.3	18.9	42.84***	50.17***
Assign a grade	49.1	32.6	20.8	44.6	33.5	41.3	41.30***	5.15
Comment on logic, organization	43.3	55.8	45.3	46.6	43.0	48.3	4.38	1.12
Pose counter arguments	17.0	19.8	20.8	25.0	20.7	9.1	5.83	14.71**
Respond with own views	7.2	11.6	13.2	11.5	9.5	7.0	7.92	2.80
Suggest related topics	14.8	16.3	27.4	21.6	22.9	8.4	9.34	14.85**

Responses	Percent of Teachers Indicating						Chi-square test	
	Stress on Information			Stress on Concepts				
	High n=277	Moderate n=86	Low n=106	High n=148	Moderate n=179	Low n=143	Information df=2	Concepts df=2
Routinely[2]								
Indicate mechanical errors	65.3	72.1	84.9	56.1	73.7	82.5	14.31***	25.78***
Suggest improvements in style	36.1	52.3	62.3	27.0	49.2	56.6	23.49***	28.41***
Point out errors of fact	59.9	74.4	63.2	64.9	60.3	65.7	5.93	1.20
Assess accuracy of conclusion	51.6	53.5	48.1	52.7	53.1	48.3	0.60	0.87
Assign a grade	69.3	72.1	71.7	66.9	69.8	75.5	0.36	2.70
Comment on logic, organization	52.7	62.8	65.1	54.1	59.2	58.7	6.08*	1.02
Pose counter arguments	30.7	39.5	46.2	38.5	34.6	35.7	8.69*	0.55
Respond with own views	18.4	32.6	44.3	24.3	28.5	27.3	27.97***	0.74
Suggest related topics	25.3	37.2	45.3	30.4	34.6	31.5	15.44***	0.73

1. Chi-square tests based on three-point scales.

2. Chi-square tests based on two-point scales.

* p < .05; ** p < .01; *** p < .001

Appendix 2: Strategies for Incorporating Writing into Content Area Instruction

Like reading, writing is a vital part of the learning process and as such deserves a place in every classroom. This bibliography lists materials to help teachers of all subjects integrate writing into their classes. The activities suggested should not only improve students' writing skills but also enhance subject-matter learning.

Following a section containing suggestions that may be used in any discipline, the entries in the bibliography are arranged according to the following subject areas: social studies, science and mathematics, physical education, vocational and business education, and English.

The entries were drawn from educational journals indexed in *Current Index to Journals in Education* and *Education Index* and from works contained in the ERIC system. ERIC documents are identified by their acquisition or "ED" numbers and may be obtained in either microfiche or paper copy from the ERIC Document Reproduction Service; for ordering information, consult a recent issue of *Resources in Education.*

General

Cunningham, Patricia M., and James W. Cunningham. (1976). SSSW, Better Content-Writing. *Clearing House* 49:5, 237–38.

Proposes a way—sustained student summary writing (SSSW)—by which content area teachers can improve students' subject learning and give them practice in writing while not expending a great deal of time in paper grading. The method is based on the techniques of sustained silent reading and requires students to spend five minutes near the end of class writing summaries of the material covered. At the end of the five-minute period, either (1) papers are collected by the teacher and corrected; (2) three students are selected to read their papers aloud; (3) students are paired with each member in a pair reading the other member's summary aloud to him or her; or (4) no follow up occurs. The procedure to be followed could be determined by a toss of a die so that daily activities vary.

Delmar, P. Jay. (1978). Composition and the High School: Steps Toward Faculty-Wide Involvement. *English Journal* 67:8, 36–38.

Outlines a technique for involving a school faculty in teaching writing and offers suggestions for writing assignments in various disciplines. Specific suggestions include writing assignments designed to develop comparison skills in a health class, the use of analysis and illustration in an art class, and the use of persuasion and analysis in a music class.

Fulwiler, Toby E. (1978). Journal Writing Across the Curriculum. ERIC Document no. ED 161 073.

120

Argues that journal writing is an expressive form of writing that teachers in all curricula can use to help their students increase writing fluency, enhance learning, and promote cognitive growth. Notes that journal writing can be assigned as homework, to begin or end a class, or to interrupt/refocus class discussion. Concludes that used in these ways, journal writing acts as a learning catalyst and as a clarifying activity that directs student attention toward a particular subject while providing writing practice and a permanent record to which the student can refer when preparing for a test or in writing a more formal composition.

Giordano, Gerard. (1978). A Modular Lesson for Writing Research Papers in Content Area Classes. ERIC Document no. ED 176 219.

Describes a modular lesson for teaching the writing of research papers in all content areas. Individual modules of the unit focus on library orientation, use of indexes, overviewing journal articles, selecting a theme article, assembling the bibliography, writing an introduction, organizing the body of the paper, citing references, and assembling a summary.

McNeil, Elton B., and Daniel N. Fader. (1967). English in Every Classroom. Final Report. ERIC Document no. ED 016 673.

Reports on a project that called upon every teacher in a school to incorporate writing and reading instruction activities into their lessons. Discusses the elements of that project, specifically, (1) the journal writing component, in which students were issued spiral notebooks in which they wrote every day and which the teacher collected once a week, but read only if requested to do so by the student (grading was based solely on the quantity of writing produced); and (2) the inclass writing component that required teachers to assign five writing exercises every two weeks, one of which was read for content and one filed in the student's folder.

Nichols, James N. (1978). Foiling Students Who'd Rather Fake It than Read It or How to Get Students to Read and Report on Books. *Journal of Reading* 22:3, 245–47.

Offers five suggestions for differing the format of the traditional book report that may be used in a variety of content areas. The five are: a test format, which calls for students to pretend to be English teachers and to make up a test over an assigned book; the letter technique, in which a student takes the role of a character in a book and writes letters to another character; the newspaper technique, which requires students to report key incidents from a book as news articles; the game format, which allows students to develop a game based on the book; and the diary or journal format in which students write about incidents from a book and their responses to the book.

Shannon, Edith, and others. (1979). How Some Teachers Teach Writing. *Today's Education* 68:3, 32–40.

Offers suggestions from teachers of social studies, English, mathematics, and science about the teaching of writing within their content areas. Suggestions include giving attention to individual needs; using the "why and because" method; teaching term paper skills; developing thinking abilities; strengthening essay writing skills; making writing important, interesting, and successful in science classes; and reviewing grammar in mathematics classes.

Smelstor, Marjorie, (ed.). (1978). A Guide to Teaching the Writing Process from Pre-Writing to Editing. ERIC Document no. ED 176 274.

Suggests activities to use in teaching the three stages of the composing process: prewriting, writing, and postwriting. Discusses the steps involved in the three stages of composition, research findings in the composing process, and student needs and instructional goals. Offers ideas for specific writing activities for use in the areas of mathematics, English, science, home economics, the fine arts, social studies, and business.

Social Studies

Alexander, Mary, and Cece Byers. (1979). Document of the Month: Writing a Letter of Appeal. *Social Education* 43:3, 198–99.

Presents an actual letter of appeal drawn from the National Archives and suggests exercises such as having students write a paraphrase of the letter that would be analyzed for clarity, style, and tone; write a similar letter; or write a paragraph discussing the letter as a historical source.

Beyer, Barry K. (1979). Pre-Writing and Rewriting to Learn. *Social Education* 43:3, 187–89.

Describes prewriting and rewriting exercises designed to help students prepare a polished social studies paper. Calls upon questioning strategies, games, simulations, and values education strategies as sources for focusing student attention on the topic.

Beyer, Barry K., and Anita Brostoff. (1979). The Time It Takes: Managing/ Evaluating Writing and Social Studies. *Social Education* 43:3, 194–97.

Suggests methods to help social studies teachers integrate writing into courses along with and instead of oral activities. Offers ideas that allow students to write to generate hypotheses for class study, to develop goals for reading, to find information, to discover new insights into a subject, to begin a class, or to end a class. Suggests ways to evaluate student writing that save teacher time.

Brostoff, Anita. (1979). Good Assignments Lead to Good Writing. *Social Education* 43:3, 184–86.

Notes that carefully designed writing assignments not only enable students to show what they have learned but also foster effective writing and learning through writing. Presents suggestions for preparing good social studies writing assignments, including defining the content and skills that students are expected to learn, devising assignments in which the level of difficulty of the task fits the level of the goal, letting students speculate on the topic, and presenting the topic in such a manner that students know what to do and how to do it.

Davis, Nelda. (1966). How to Work with the Academically Talented in the Social Studies. How to Do It Series, Number 21. ERIC Document no. ED 083 055.

Provides suggestions for dealing with academically talented students in social studies classes. Recommends using an unsolved problem of history to interest students in preparing research papers. Suggested topics include the intention of the framers of the Sherman antitrust law in regard to labor unions, the safety-valve theory in regard to western lands, the role of Mrs. Surratt in the Lincoln assassination, and the motivation behind the activities of John D. Rockefeller.

Giroux, Henry A. (1979). Teaching Content and Thinking through Writing. *Social Education* 43:3, 190-93.

Offers a procedure that actively involves students in discussing, analyzing, and writing about social studies course content. The activity requires several class periods and uses material from a standard textbook. Its intent is to familiarize students with the concepts of "organizing idea" and "frame of reference" and calls upon them to organize paragraphs supporting a given idea by using pieces of information drawn from their reading.

Klasky, Charles. (1979). World Geography—Believe It or Not! *Social Education* 43:1, 34-35.

Describes a week-long geography project based on Ripley's *Believe It or Not* books that helps students develop a greater understanding of different cultures. Students spend three days researching unusual or different cultures and two days writing and assembling a booklet on some aspect of their research. Contends that the assignment forces students to decide what is "unusual" or interesting and promotes discussions of ethnocentrism, causing students to examine their own values and prejudices.

Niskayuna Central School District 1, Schenectady, New York. (1979). Integration of Content and Problem Solving Skills. ERIC Document no. ED 179 479.

Designed to help teachers learn how to integrate content and problem solving skills in the social studies curriculum. Problem solving skills include analyzing an in-depth question/problem, selecting a format for recording information, gathering and recording information, and writing a summary. Presents student analysis of a question that involved labeling nouns, verbs, and limiters; defining unfamiliar words; and restating the question.

Petrini, Glenda C. (1976). Teach Johnny How to Write for Social Studies Essay Tests. *Clearing House* 49:9, 394-96.

Advances a technique for teaching social studies students to write that is based on Harold Herber's *Teaching Reading in the Content Areas* and on the Umbrella Form of paragraph organization devised by Dorothy Rich. The exercise familiarizes students with the writing patterns of cause/effect, compare/contrast, chronology, main idea/detail, and enumeration compositions. It requires students to write five-sentence paragraphs, each with a topic sentence; three sentences supplying proofs, details, examples, or reasons; and a concluding sentence.

Rivers, Larry E. (1979). Indentured Servitude in Colonial America: Teaching Social Studies and the Basic Skills. *Social Education* 43:3, 214-17.

Presents a two-day lesson integrating the basic skills of reading, writing, and critical thinking with social studies content. The lesson requires students to list information they have gathered, write a main idea, and then write a well-structured paragraph based on rewriting exercises.

Van Nostrand, A. D. (1979). Writing and the Generation of Knowledge. *Social Education* 43:3, 178-80.

Contends that a student gains knowledge through the act of writing as he or she joins bits of information into a whole. Presents a model for scanning students' written material to determine the ways ideas are related. Notes that the value of a piece of information depends on how the writer joins it with other information.

Ventre, Raymond. (1979). Developmental Writing: Social Studies Assignments. *Social Education* 43:3, 181–83, 197.

Presents guidelines for developmental writing in social studies and a sample assignment that involves writing letters about historical figures. Suggests that the letters be critiqued by three student peers and that the critiques stress the writer's ideas. Discusses the relationship between the thinking process and the writing process and the need to break these processes into manageable units for students.

Science and Mathematics

Davies, Brian. (1976). Physics Lectures and Student Notes. *Physics Education* 11:1, 33–36.

Relates a strategy that allows teachers to rate their effectiveness by examining their students' lecture notes, which the students have recorded on carbon paper. Contends that through this technique teachers are able to determine communication problems that may occur.

Donlan, Dan. (1975). Science Writing: A Call for Continuing Education. *Science Teacher* 42:10, 19–20.

Suggests that science teachers introduce students to the variety of styles appropriate to writing reports of a historical, analytical, descriptive, or biographical nature. Proposes that teachers use a method of diagramming of paragraphs to show students how material is organized from a topic sentence. Advocates the use of more than one source or of controlled sources for reports in order to promote student originality in writing.

Ellman, Neil. (1978). Science in the English Classroom. *English Journal* 67:4, 63–65.

Argues for an interdisciplinary approach to instruction. Lists five ways of increasing interpersonal contact among faculty members and offers suggestions for reading and writing assignments that would integrate science and English instruction. Writing suggestions include having students write conversations with or letters to famous inventors, letters to the editor about problems caused by technology, mystery stories in which the solution depends on a scientific principle, and futuristic scenarios.

Geeslin, William. (1977). Using Writing about Mathematics as a Teaching Technique. *Mathematics Teacher* 70:2, 112–15.

Proposes a technique for writing about mathematical concepts as a means of increasing student understanding of those concepts. The technique involves the gradual introduction of writing into assignments and has students explain in one or two sentences how addition and subtraction are related, then write a paragraph or two discussing a single concept, and, finally, write about the relationship between two concepts such as equation/graph, line/plane, circle/ellipse, or point/line.

Maxwell, Rhoda, and Stephen Judy. (1978). Science Writing in the English Classroom. *English Journal* 67:4, 78–81.

Reports on a team teaching project that was designed to integrate science writing and creative writing by having students prepare books on scientific topics in an imaginative manner.

Reid, H. Kay, and Glenn McGlathery. (1977). Science and Creative Writing. *Science and Children* 14:4, 19–20.

Contains a list of thirty-three creative writing activities that can be coordinated with various elementary or middle school science units. The activities include studying clouds and writing about what is seen, writing the history of earth from the perspective of a being from outer space, and writing about the needs and feelings of a jungle animal that has been placed in a new environment.

Schlenker, Richard M., and Constance M. Perry. (1979). A Writing Guide for Student Oceanography Laboratory and Field Research Reports. ERIC Document no. ED 178 332.

Presents activities designed to improve the writing and composition skills of oceanography (or other science) students. Provides suggestions for keeping a field notebook and offers a format for the preparation of a research paper.

Shapland, Jeff, and Phil Watson. (1976). Beyond the Worksheet. *Times Educational Supplement* n3199, 20–21 (24 September 1976).

Contends that the act of writing about ideas that are important to students is of greater importance to their learning than filling out worksheets and proposes the use of a chemistry journal in which students write about their activities and the ideas they have come across. Notes that, apart from the direct benefits of such writing, the journals can be used to assess student strengths and weaknesses more clearly than can worksheets.

Wilkes, John. (1978). Science Writing: Who? What? How? *English Journal* 67:8, 56–60.

Proposes the use of written dialogues as a means of developing the writing skills of science students. The dialogues dramatize conversations about scientific developments and involve a scientist and an intelligent, eager-to-learn listener.

Zimmerman, S. Scott. (1978). Writing for Chemistry: Food for Thought Must Be Appetizing. *Journal of Chemical Education* 55:11, 727.

Presents several suggestions for improving the technical writing skills of students in chemistry that range from organizing a first draft through preparing a final revision.

Physical Education

Georgia State Department of Education, Atlanta. Office of Instructional Services. (1978). A Reading Program for the 70s: Physical Education. ERIC Document no. ED 166 660.

Describes activities that promote perceptual motor development and that link language arts experiences. Among the writing activities for students in grades six through eight are making a sports dictionary, writing about the characteristics of sports figures, and writing about various aspects of physical education.

Metcalf, James. (1979). Teaching Writing in Physical Education. *Journal of Physical Education and Recreation* 50:9, 38.

Argues that physical education offers many untapped opportunities for teaching writing and for making students feel good about writing. Notes that motor experiences and somatic sensations are peculiar to that discipline and that these experiences and sensations can provide rich sources of writing topics. Suggestions for integrating writing into the physical education classroom include: assigning each student to a writing group so that writing can be shared, making writing assignments short and unstructured, responding to student writing to show that it is valued, having students revise their work, encouraging students to keep their work, showing an interest in one's own development as a writer, and encouraging colleagues to join in the effort.

Turner, Bud. (1977). PE Journal. *Journal of Physical Education and Recreation* 48:5, 56–7.

Reports on a journal writing activity in which students write about the goals they want to reach in physical education and the activities they are to take part in as they strive for those goals. The journals consist of manila folders containing activity sheets, each of which provides space for the students to write about key words they have learned during an acitivty, accomplishments they are most proud of, and books or magazine articles they have read on a particular activity.

Vocational and Business Education

Handorf, James L., and Donald A. Nelson. (1970). Student Success with Creative Composition. *Business Education Forum* 25:2, 10.

Reports that the use of statements that encourage creativity as prompts to composing at the typewriter achieve more positive responses from students in typing classes than traditional prompts. Sample assignments include having students write about how they would feel if they were an object or an animal, complete "what if . . ." statements, and respond to letters to "Dear Abby."

McLeod, Alan. (1978). Stimulating Writing through Job Awareness. *English Journal* 67:8, 42–43.

Suggests thirty-four oral and written activities involving jobs that can be used to motivate students to write, including responding to want ads in newspapers, writing letters of recommendation, exploring the impact of oral and written language on prospective employers, writing newspaper stories about people and jobs, and writing autobiographies emphasizing employment.

Turner, Thomas N. (1979). A Stylish Wedding: Infusing Career Education into Creative Writing and Composition. *English Journal* 68:7, 59–62.

Lists fifty activities that permit career education students to learn about a specific field in which they have an interest as well as to use their creative and expository writing skills. Specific suggestions include writing job descriptions of real or fantasy jobs, writing letters from the point of view of fictional characters about their career needs, and writing a script for a job interview between an employer and a prospective employee who have a personality conflict.

Williams, Wayne. (1976). Oh No! Not Another Term Paper—A Research Assignment in Economics. *Balance Sheet* 58:3, 117, 139.

Outlines projects that have been particularly successful in bridging the gap between classroom economics knowledge and community activities. Writing assignments include having students discover and write about how local businesses are affected by current economic conditions, write a history of a local business, assess the value of mass transit, examine the question of penal reform, and examine the local system for urban planning.

Winger, Fred. (1975). Typewriting Composition Projects with an Occupational Thrust. *Business Education Forum* 29:7, 6–7.

Lists thirteen projects that encourage thinking and composing at the typewriter. Among the projects are three that call for students to write compositions justifying their presence in a typing class, to analyze the ways in which businesses would be affected if the typewriter did not exist, and to research and write about whether the number of clerks and secretaries will decrease in the future.

Zimpfer, Forest. (1976). Typewriting: A Model for Building Composition Skill. *Business Education Forum* 31:2, 14–16.

Presents teaching techniques and a model to improve writing skills as well as typing skills. Various assignments call for students to compose personal essays, compile research papers, and write job application letters. Topics are supplied by the teacher and are based on student interest.

English

Benson, Marion. (1977–78). Poetry as a Stimulus to Writing. *English Quarterly* 10:4, 45–53.

Presents a technique that uses students' responses to poetry as a tool for developing writing skills and literature appreciation. Activities include having students write about personal experiences to illustrate the main idea of a poem; having them explain how elements such as simile, metaphor, alliteration, and allusion contribute to the expression of an experience; calling for critical interpretation addressed to specific points about a poem; assigning comparison and contrast themes; and having students write their own poems.

Bramer, Mary. (1975). With Thanks to Edgar Lee Masters. *English Journal* 64:6, 39–40.

Describes a poetry writing project that called for students to research local historical figures and write their epitaphs in the style of Edgar Lee Masters' *Spoon River Anthology*.

Carlisle, Elizabeth, and Judithe Speidel. (1979). Local History as a Stimulus for Writing. *English Journal* 68:5, 55–57.

Details a humanities course that was designed with a focus on careful, precise observation as the basis for increasing understanding and for producing effective writing. Describes the major assignment, which required the students to imagine that they were historical characters from their hometown and to keep journals of their daily activities. Reports that such writing engaged many facets of the students' lives, including their sense impressions, emotions, intellectual curiosity, and fantasies.

Foster, Mary Ellen. (1976). Design in Art and Literature: Drawing Students into Writing. *English Journal* 65:6, 64–67.

Describes a strategy that allowed students to use a project in design as a means of improving their writing and of understanding the writing process. The technique involved having students design a toy, game, recipe, tool, or dance and then write about the process of creating the design. It also involved having them use the letters of their names to learn that letters and words have a design, and then extending this to show that stories and poems also have an underlying shape.

Hyland, Gary. (1977). Accreditation Ideas. *English Quarterly* 10:1, 55–72.

Lists teaching ideas for various aspects of English and the language arts. Among the writing ideas are: have students write narratives in which ordinary objects from around the house become clues for a mystery or aids for escaping from prison, set up a situation in which someone has to write in order to communicate with others, explain denotation and connotation and then have students rewrite a neutral paragraph with a specific connotation, have students write descriptions of commonplace objects without mentioning their name or function, and have students select three magazine pictures and use them as reference points around which to build a short story. Also offers suggestions on evaluating student work and optional creative writing assignments.

Insel, Deborah. (1975). Foxfire in the City. *English Journal* 64:6, 36–38.

Describes a "Foxfire"-inspired project that allowed high school students in an urban area to write a social history of their community drawn from information obtained in interviews with senior citizens in the community.

Kahl, Marilyn, and others. (1976). Potpourri '76: A Collection of Teaching Ideas for Elementary and Secondary Schools. ERIC Document no. ED 131 479.

Offers a variety of suggestions for writing assignments including having students keep "psychological logs" that recreate the three main processes involved in the creation of a work of art, write dialogue, create a conversation with William Shakespeare or write about the contributions of a minor character to one of his plays, write a critical analysis of *Great Expectations*, write short stories, and write autobiographies.

Kitzhaber, Albert R. (1966). Twentieth Century Lyrics. Science and Poetry. Literature Curriculum IV, Student Version. ERIC Document no. ED 010 819.

Presents materials for use in teaching modern poetry and in comparing it to scientific writings. Discusses the similarities and differences between scientists and poets in their approach to experience. Offers several writing assignments that illustrate each's point of view, including having students research and write about various scientists' use of imagination that led them to make important discoveries; write about Shelley's use of scientific facts in his poem, "The Cloud"; write a paragraph from an objective point of view and then from a subjective point of view; and write a description of an object (a rose, a sea shell) as a scientist would see it and then as a poet might see it.

Kohl, Herb. (1978). Imaginary Voyages. *Teacher* 95:6, 12-19.

Advances an approach that uses themes arising from childhood fantasies and imaginary voyages for developing writing and discussion skills in elementary (or older) children. Suggests the reading of *Don Quixote, Gulliver's Travels, The Odyssey, Pilgrim's Progress,* and the myth of Orpheus to stimulate writing and discussion.

Laubach, David. (1979). Beyond Foxfire. *English Journal* 68:5, 52-54.

Extends the Foxfire concept of collecting and writing folklore and cultural history to include analyzing the material collected to determine what it says about the folk group, what it says about the informant, and the possible symbolic or unconscious ideas embodied in the lore. Lists twelve possible projects, including: collecting and writing about a series of folk beliefs, legends, or ethnic jokes from a single informant or from an occupational folk group; finding and writing about local crafts-people who still practice traditional methods; writing short sketches with a great deal of dialect or a dramatic scene in which the folk speech of a particular group is captured; writing a poem or short story based on a folk superstition; and writing a fictionalized sketch in which a particular folk group is shown celebrating a holiday or enjoying an annual event that is peculiar to that group.

Lowery, Skip. (1978). The Photography Connection: Picture Taking and the Craft of Writing. *Media and Methods* 14:8, 69-72.

Reports on a teaching approach that calls upon the language of photography to help students become more proficient writers. Stresses that like a good photograph good writing takes time and skill and that like a good photograph a good essay makes an abstract idea concrete and the ordinary important.

Moore, Joseph B. (1978). A Writing Week. *English Journal* 67:8, 39-41.

Demonstrates how students might be asked to write in class instead of doing routine drills. Provides the following outline of lessons in preparing a composition: Monday: students brainstorm for ideas, choose topics, and work on first draft; Tuesday: students continue work on first draft; Wednesday: students read each other's first drafts and each student is given one paper to take home and evaluate in one paragraph; Thursday: students discuss their evaluations with the evaluators and begin second draft; Friday: students discuss their work and begin third draft.

Raybin, Ron. (1970). The Technique of the Infelicitous Alternative. ERIC Document no. ED 049 249.

Proposes changing crucial characteristics of a literary work and presenting students with unsuitable alternatives as an effective means of leading them to the discovery of the artistic appropriateness of the original. Suggestions for use in teaching composition include: having the class discuss dittoed paragraphs that ineffectively repeat words and phrases to illustrate the importance of variety in writing style; having the class write intentionally disorganized paragraphs to discover what coherence or unity is; and teaching the importance of transition by altering or removing them from sample paragraphs.

Small, Robert, Jr. (1979). The YA Novel in the Composition Program, Part II. *English Journal* 68:7, 75–77.

Presents more than sixty ways to use the young adult novel to enrich the composition program, including having students choose the books they would most like to have with them if they were stranded on a desert island and explain their choices, write book reviews from another person's viewpoint, and write scenes in which the main characters from two novels meet.

Treeson, Ruth H. (1978). Keeping the Arts in Language Arts. *Curriculum Review* 17:3, 189–92.

Argues that bringing the arts into the English classroom will help students to rediscover within themselves the ability to share their own experiences, thoughts, and feelings in writing. Delineates a teaching approach that uses songs and photographs to teach description, narration, techniques of organization and of style, argument, exposition, and point of view.

Wiseman, Nell. (1979). A Unit for Writing Children's Stories. *English Journal* 68:5, 47–49.

Describes a six-week unit on writing children's stories that was successful in motivating high school students to write and in increasing their awareness of audience. Discusses the weekly activities involved, including having the students recall their own favorite children's books and stories, having them read a variety of children's literature, arranging to have the students visit elementary school classes and read published stories during story hour, and having students prepare a final version of their own stories for reading to the elementary school students.